MATAKANA

A RANDOM HOUSE BOOK published by
Random House New Zealand
18 Poland Road, Glenfield, Auckland, New Zealand
For more information about our titles go to
www.randomhouse.co.nz

A catalogue record for this book is available from
the National Library of New Zealand

First published 2008

ISBN 978 1 86979 038 7

Design: Karryn Muschamp
Printed in China by South China Printing Co Ltd

The author is grateful for the assistance of the
Rodney Economic Development Trust

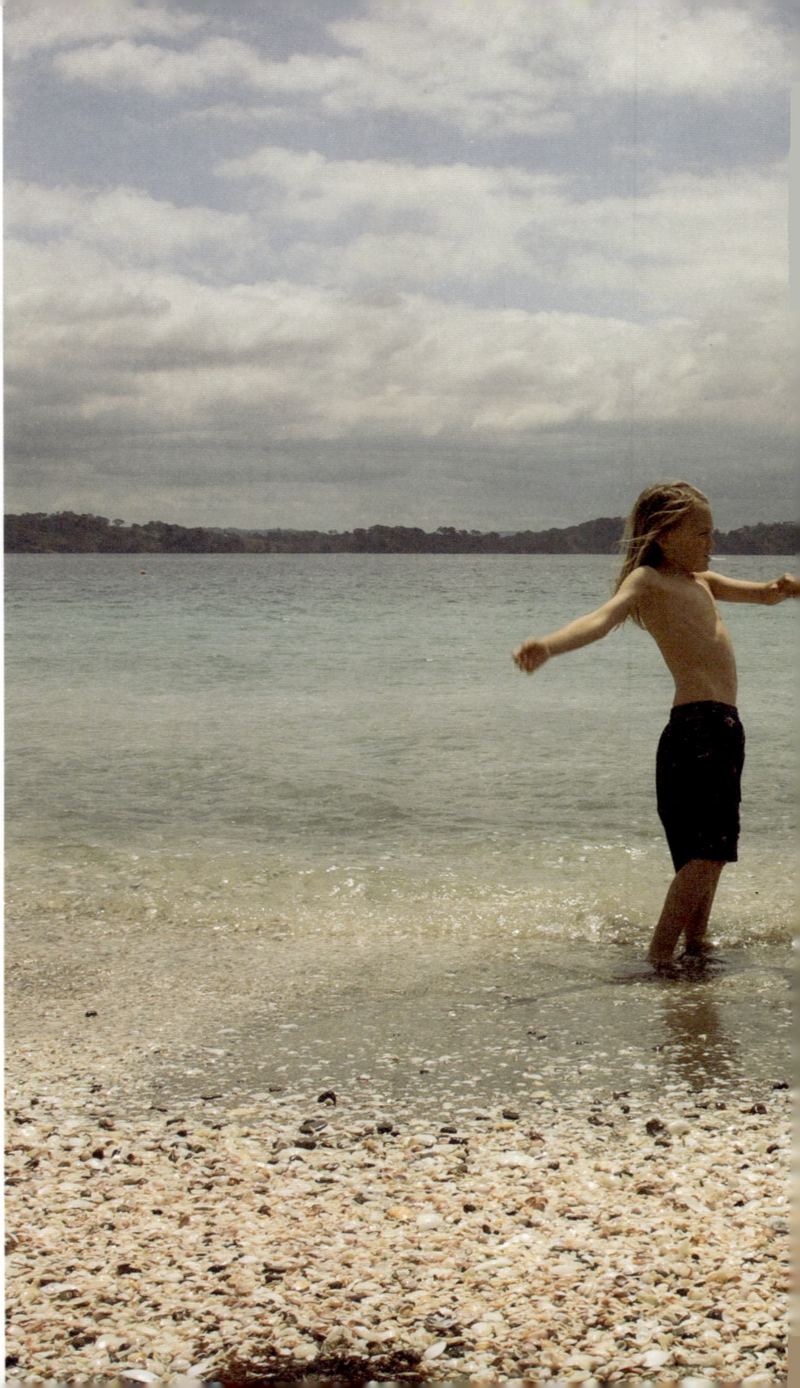

MATAKANA

LAURAINE JACOBS   Photography by KEN DOWNIE

RANDOM HOUSE
NEW ZEALAND

OPPOSITE: First
World War memorial,
Matakana Village

CONTENTS

INTRODUCTION

As a small child, I was frequently taken by my parents to stay with friends at a private bay on the Takatu Peninsula in the Matakana region. We would stop and buy *The New Zealand Herald* and ice-creams at the general store in the one-shop town of Matakana, and then head out on the dusty, winding road to Christian Bay. I can remember looking from the top of the ridge at the unspoilt sweep of land below, the Omaha Beach spit. It was accessible only by boat or over private farmland at the time. No causeway, no groynes to protect the beach and no holiday homes. To me, that epitomised New Zealand — a remote, unspoilt beach with even sets of waves crashing onto the sand. I had no idea I would live on the edge of that beach almost 50 years later. And no clue the region would produce everything a keen cook like me would need and want to create delicious meals.

There have been other connections to Matakana through the years. When our children were young we regularly took them sailing on our yacht, and our favourite destination was Kawau Island, as its Bon Accord Harbour is a safe haven in almost any weather. We explored the coastline, anchoring in Mahurangi Harbour and at Leigh, and caught fish, scallops and crayfish. Once our children grew up we spent several holidays with friends on the beachfront at Omaha, loving the sandy beach and the golf course and tasting the terrific produce growing in the vicinity.

Our close friends Richard and Christine Didsbury also introduced us to Matakana more than 20 years ago when they first holidayed in a caravan at their newly purchased farm at Brick Bay, and shared their vision and plans for the Matakana farmers' market and the Village complex.

OPPOSITE: In my
Omaha kitchen, ready
to cook from the
farmers' market

For me, the best change over the time I have been involved with the area has been the establishment and growth of the market. I love the idea of artisan producers and growers meeting and talking with their customers, and regard the development of farmers' markets as the most significant advancement in the New Zealand food world during the 20 years I have written about the subject. My Saturdays would not be the same without my early-morning visit to the market.

The area has always been a haven for lifestylers, growers and vintners, and the farmers' market and the new retail centre, Matakana Village, have been a great boon to producers, cooks and growers. Day visitors, overseas tourists and holidaymakers are all attracted to Matakana with its wealth of wineries, cafés and restaurants. And an increasing number of city-dwellers are giving up the traffic jams and densely populated residential areas to re-establish their lives in the rural atmosphere of this exciting, developing region.

The area surrounding Matakana's heart, the Village, is mostly pleasant rolling countryside with occasional pockets of houses in small communities, and it's filled with an enormous range of things to do. The coastline is gentle, sometimes spectacular, with hidden coves and beaches where you can get away from the crowds.

This book is not intended to be an official and all-encompassing guide to the region, but rather it is to provide a taste of the food, wine and pleasures of the area that I have grown to love.

FROM THE BEGINNING

The Matakana Anglican church, built in 1914

As far back as the seventeenth century, the coastal area around Matakana was occupied by two tribes, Ngai Tahuhu and Ngati Tai. No doubt they feasted on the harvest from the rich seafood beds around Omaha and Kawau bays and on the abundant fish found in the waterways of the Mahurangi and Matakana rivers.

Over the next century, right through to the Waikato War in 1863, the region was fiercely fought over by different sub-tribes and travelling groups from the Te Kawerau people, the Marutuahu Confederation, the Hauraki tribes, Ngati Paoa, Ngapuhi and Ngati Whatua. These skirmishes and battles, which were especially common during the annual shark-fishing season, changed the patterns of tribal domination in the area, and there was often loss of life.

The arrival of the first Europeans in the 1820s led to a restless situation that lasted for several decades. The Ngati Raupo occupied the Tawharanui area, while the Ngati Manuhiri occupied the area from Omaha to Pakiri. In 1841 a large tract of land known as the Mahurangi Purchase, stretching from Takapuna in the south to Te Arai Point, was bought by the Crown and was opened up for Pakeha settlement. In 1844, 42 Europeans were residing in the Matakana area. Kauri was abundant in the region and by 1846 pastoral and timber licences were being issued, disputed and protested about by local Maori. The rivers made it easy to transport timber to Auckland. By 1853 a sawmill was operating on the site that is today occupied by the farmers' market and the Village shops.

In the Matakana district, where the survey and division of available land for settlement was not completed until 1858, many lots were settled by free grants. Skilled colonists were sought in Britain, and although successful applicants had to pay for their passage, they could select their own parcel of land on arrival. Having a wife entitled a male settler to an extra 40 acres. Once they had successfully farmed their land for a period of about five years, they would be given title. Those early farms in Matakana were mostly mixed, raising crops and animals.

In the 1850s the largest orchard in the country was established on the Matthews' property near Omaha, with seeds and cuttings collected from around the world. Their plant nursery, which lasted until 1880, supplied stock for Governor Sir George Grey's extensive and important gardens at Mansion House on Kawau Island.

The first public buildings, a church and a school, were erected at Matakana in early 1862. By 1865 the school was attended by 20 children, who often journeyed long, difficult distances for their education. In 1868 the first store, which also served as a post office, opened and by 1875 there was a small library.

Through the period from 1863 to the mid-1880s gumdiggers and kauri-loggers worked the area around Matakana, and by 1886 the giant kauri were almost completely felled. Fruit growing, particularly citrus, then became an important industry, with boatloads of the crops being sent to Auckland, but by the turn of the century most local orchards had been converted into dairy farms.

Shipbuilding was also an established local industry at this time, with several builders setting up important yards in and around Matakana and the Mahurangi. The only reliable way to travel to and from the region was by boat up and down the coast. In the 1870s there was a weekly boat service connecting Matakana with Auckland which took local produce to the markets.

Despite the notion of a 'Great North Road' being mooted by early provincial government and £2000 being granted for its construction in 1855, the area was mainly without roads throughout most of the nineteenth century. This proposed road remained a firm line on the map, but the rugged countryside and bush between Auckland and Whangarei to the north made it difficult to build and maintain what was then no more than a roughly cut track. It was occasionally passable by dray, but was frequently overgrown or washed out. It was not until the turn of the century that road access to the north became possible.

In 1902 the dairy factory opened in Matakana. It still stands today, next to the tiny church, St Leonard's, built in 1914 in the centre of the village. The post office opposite also dates from this time. By 1930 the pupils of the district school had outgrown their building so another site was found and a new building erected.

Tourism, one of the mainstays of Matakana today, has always been a part
of the district's livelihood. As early as the 1890s visitors would come to view
the ornamental gardens established by the Matthews brothers at Omaha. Once
road transport opened up the area in the mid-1930s the Matakana boarding
house provided accommodation and meals for travellers, as the return journey
from Auckland took longer than a day.

In 1936 electric power was connected to the area, but two years later extensive
flooding set back the district as bridges and culverts were washed away.
During the Second World War three camps were set up around Matakana to
house some of the 60,000 American troops based in New Zealand.

A hardware business was established by local builders Percy Smith and
Norman Roke in the 1950s and merged with the Matakana Timber Centre
in 1989. The Matakana Dairy Company went the way of many small
companies when it amalgamated with the Rodney Dairy Company in 1963
and its offices were transferred to Warkworth.

In the late 1970s Anthony and Sue Morris established their pottery, Morris
& James, near the centre of Matakana, giving tourists another reason to
visit the region. This was closely followed by the growth of viticulture and
winemaking throughout Matakana and the surrounding areas, attracting
a flood of visitors and interest in the region. Wine had been produced in the
area as early as 1866, from peaches, and also in the 1940s when Russian
immigrant Alexis Migounoff made his Lemora wine from lemon and orange
juice at his Matakana orchard. The Vuletic brothers revived winemaking at
their Antipodean vineyard when they planted their vines at Tongue Farm Rd
in 1970, to be followed in 1988 by the establishment of Mary Evans and David
Hoskins' Heron's Flight vineyard. Many others have followed and several
vineyards now have tastings and serve food at their cellar doors.

With the purchase of the Matakana timberyard by the Brick Bay Trust, and
the construction of the farmers' market, Matakana Village shops and cinema
on the site, and the blossoming of accommodation, restaurants and cafés and
other attractions in the region, the future of Matakana is exciting.

FRESH FROM THE FARM

Open every Saturday from 8am to 1pm, year round, the Matakana farmers' market has a wonderful atmosphere as locals and visitors mingle to talk, taste and buy local produce. Operated by the Brick Bay Trust, it is unusual among New Zealand farmers' markets in that it has a permanent, dedicated structure and a certified kitchen so that food can be produced on site.

The market, behind the Matakana Village and Cinemas, is in a picturesque setting. A small river flows by on the boundary and rustic wooden stalls have brick- and cream-coloured striped awnings to shelter the stallholders from the summer sunshine and occasional rain showers.

Tables with umbrellas provide shaded seating and the market operates a clever rubbish system that separates recyclable waste. Generally a local musician or group provides entertainment and background music for shoppers. Those in the know arrive early to catch the best produce from a huge variety of local farmers and growers, many of whom have had stalls there since the market's inception.

You can find locally grown fruits such as blueberries, tomatoes, citrus, grapes, strawberries and other seasonal specialities that appear for short periods. There is always an amazing array of seasonal vegetables, including a dedicated stall of Asian herbs and vegetables. Other fresh produce includes oysters, free-range eggs, floral honeys, bags of freshly mixed salads, flowers and plants. Some of the stallholders take advantage of local produce to make added-value products like mustards, jams and jellies, preserves, chocolates, olive oils, preserved meats and terrines, smoked fish and vegetables, superb fresh breads and pastries, and more. Each week there's bound to be something new and exciting that most visitors will not have seen or tried before.

There's also plenty of ready-to-eat food at the market and dishes to take home. Whitebait and mussel fritters are popular, and there is a whole range of other delicious hot food to try. With a commercial kitchen on site there's a great line-up of cooks plying hungry appetites with breakfast rolls, hot sausages, tasty Italian food — all cooked on the spot. And the line for coffee grows longer and longer throughout the morning.

A word of warning: I can always distinguish the true farmers' market shoppers from the tourists by the bags they carry. The market is a plastic-free zone and no regular visitor would dream of coming without several 'green' bags to carry their purchases home.

COOKING FROM THE MARKET

OPPOSITE: Shopping for food to cook for lunch

The following recipes are all inspired by the great produce I buy each week at the Matakana farmers' market. Saturday morning is a really special time for me. I'm up early year round so I can be at the market by 8am when it opens. It's my chance to connect with the growers and artisan producers and see what they've brought to sell each week.

The joy of fresh seasonal produce — picked dotted with dew or with the dirt still clinging to the roots, eggs so freshly laid they are still warm, or a new product that has been developed — is truly inspirational for a cook. And I love the single-shot latte waiting for me, made to my idiosyncratic tastes.

Here are recipes for five starters, five main courses, five salad and vegetable dishes and five desserts, all of which were first made in my Omaha Beach kitchen upon my return from the market and have become family favourites. I usually spread all my newly bought produce across the bench and that's when the ideas really start to flow.

The recipes here are simple — simple to make, simple to eat and the sort of food that makes everyone happy. My sort of food.

COURGETTE AND FETA FRITTERS

Throughout the summer courgettes are a staple in the farmers' market and at the roadside stalls in Matakana. The fresh mint in these fritters really lifts the flavour and goes well with the feta. Try to choose fresh, firm young courgettes as they contain less water, which dilutes the batter. I love to serve these tiny fritters with drinks. They're a great match for chilled pinot gris.

Makes about 20 small fritters

Wine match
Pinot gris

4 firm courgettes, grated
4 eggs
2 tablespoons flour
small pinch of ground cumin
salt and freshly ground black pepper
150g soft feta, chopped into small cubes or crumbled
3 tablespoons chopped dill
4–5 tablespoons olive or light vegetable oil
lemon wedges, to serve

Place the grated courgette in a sieve over a bowl and allow any excess water to drain away.

Beat the eggs in a bowl with the flour, cumin and seasoning to make a smooth batter. Mix in the courgettes, feta and dill.

Heat a heavy-based frying pan and moisten the surface with 1–2 tablespoons of oil per batch. When the pan is hot reduce the heat slightly and drop in tablespoonfuls of the batter, 4–5 at a time, and fry over gentle heat until golden on each side. Place on paper towels to absorb any excess oil. Serve at once with lemon wedges.

The fritters can be kept warm by covering with tinfoil, but are best eaten straight away.

SPINACH AND SAUSAGE FRITTATA

We're so lucky to be able to buy Greg Scopas' terrific Salumeria Fontana sausages at the Matakana market, along with his range of bacon and other cured meats. I love them all, but my favourites are the Sicilian-style sweet fennel sausages made from pure pork. The other essential ingredient for this frittata are the bright-yellow-yolked eggs I buy from Jeni Quayle of Waybyond Organics. I like to make this frittata in a frying pan that can go in the oven so the top can be nicely browned under the grill. Try serving this with sauvignon blanc.

Serves 4–6

Wine match
Sauvignon blanc

8 Sicilian-style sweet fennel sausages
  (or other tasty sausages)
1 tablespoon olive oil
3–4 cups baby spinach leaves, washed
2 large onions, finely sliced
1 cup chopped fresh herbs (such as
  thyme, basil and parsley)
8 free-range organic eggs
salt and freshly ground black pepper
100g tasty cheddar, grated

Preheat the oven to 175°C.

Fry the sausages in olive oil in a heavy frying pan until golden brown all over. Remove from the pan. When cool, cut each sausage into several pieces.

If there is more than 2–3 tablespoons of fat in the frying pan, tip some out. Lower the heat, add the spinach to the pan and cook until wilted. Remove from the pan and set aside to cool. Add the onions to the pan and fry very gently until soft, golden and nutty (about 15 minutes).

Spread the onions evenly over the base of the frying pan. Scatter half the herbs over the onions, place the sausage pieces evenly on top, then make a final layer with the spinach.

Beat the eggs with the salt and pepper and pour over the vegetables. Top with the remaining herbs and the grated cheese and cook for about 2 minutes over very low heat. Place the pan in the oven for 3–4 minutes, then switch on the grill to brown the top. Serve warm or cold, accompanied by spicy chutney.

PASTA WITH SMOKED SALMON, BEANS AND CORN

Pete Clementson's produce from his Matakana Smokehouse is a recent and welcome addition to the Matakana farmers' market. Pete smokes salmon and a variety of vegetables. Here I have used his salmon and some summery vegetables, tossed together to serve with pappardelle. This simple dish relies on fresh tastes and takes a minimum of fuss to prepare.

Serves 4

Wine match
A fruity
gewürztraminer

2 cobs sweetcorn
250g snowbeans, topped and sliced
250g dried pappardelle
4 tablespoons extra virgin olive oil
300g hot-smoked salmon, broken into chunks
4 tablespoons chopped fresh summer herbs (such as parsley, basil and tarragon)
grated zest and juice of 1 lemon
salt and freshly ground black pepper

Bring a large saucepan of salted water to the boil, add the corn and simmer for 10 minutes until tender. Drain and allow the corn to cool a little, then cut the kernels from the cobs with a sharp knife. Reserve the kernels and discard the cobs.

Bring a small saucepan of salted water to a simmer and add the beans. Simmer for 3–4 minutes until just tender, then immediately refresh under cold running water so they retain their lovely green colour. Reserve.

Cook the pasta in plenty of well-salted boiling water according to the instructions on the packet. When the pasta is al dente, drain and return to the hot pan with the olive oil. Toss well, then divide among 4 heated plates. Toss the corn, beans, salmon and herbs with the lemon zest and juice. Season with salt and plenty of freshly ground black pepper and serve over the pasta immediately.

POTATO, FENNEL, FETA, OLIVE AND LEMON TART

I keep several blocks of puff pastry in my freezer at Omaha so I can whip up a tart for a lunch dish or a great starter for friends who pop in unexpectedly. All sorts of interesting things from the garden or the store cupboard can be used as toppings. This tart, which I first made when I cooked lunch for broadcaster John Campbell, who came to our house at Omaha to interview writer Michael Pollan, is now voted by my family and friends as their favourite.

Serves 6 as a meal with salad or makes up to 24 pieces as a pre-dinner snack

Wine match
Rosé

500g puff pastry
3 large Agria potatoes, peeled and cut
   into 1.5cm slices
1 egg, beaten
3 bulbs fennel, sliced paper thin
2 teaspoons fennel seeds
150g crumbly feta
½ cup black olives, preferably pitted
peel of 1 preserved lemon, cut into
   small dice
sea salt and freshly ground black pepper
small bunch flat-leafed parsley,
   leaves only

Roll out the pastry to fit a 30cm x 40cm oven tray. Allow the pastry to rest in the refrigerator for at least 30 minutes. Preheat the oven to 200°C.

Simmer the potatoes in boiling salted water until tender. Drain well and set aside to cool.

Brush the whole surface of the pastry with the beaten egg, then spread the potato slices on top. Brush the potatoes with any leftover egg.

Layer the fennel on top of the potatoes and scatter the seeds over. Crumble the feta over next, then dot with olives and preserved lemon dice. Season with salt and pepper.

Place in the oven and turn the heat up an extra 10°C so the pastry really starts to cook. When the pastry is puffed and golden brown on the edges and underside (this should take about 20 minutes, but will depend on your oven), remove the tart from the oven. Scatter the parsley leaves over and cut into generous wedges to serve.

GRILLED OYSTERS WITH SPICY TOPPING

Orata Marine Farms sell lovely briny Pacific oysters at the Matakana farmers' market to take home and freshly shuck. They are superb served *au naturel* straight from the shell with wedges of lemon, but when we've eaten our fill (can you ever have too many oysters?) I will whip up this buttery topping and lightly grill them. Lovely with pinot gris.

Makes 24

Wine match
Pinot gris

100g butter, softened
2 cloves garlic, crushed
1 teaspoon curry powder
4 tablespoons chopped coriander, plus extra sprigs for garnish
24 freshly shucked oysters on the half-shell
lemon wedges, to serve

Preheat the grill.

Beat the butter, garlic, curry powder and coriander until well combined. Place ½ teaspoon of this butter on top of each oyster and place under the grill until the butter melts and the oysters are gently set. Garnish with extra sprigs of coriander and serve with lemon wedges.

SPICED GRILLED FISH WITH STEWED RED CAPSICUMS WITH TOMATO AND BASIL

There is always a stall at the Matakana farmers' market stocked with colourful capsicums and other vegetables. I like to cook the ripe capsicums long and slowly to bring out their wonderful sweetness. Here I've added fresh tomato and basil to capture flavours reminiscent of late summer — a perfect accompaniment for freshly caught fish. Leigh Fisheries processes some of New Zealand's finest fish for export and for top restaurants at home, including the Leigh Sawmill Café.

Serves 4–6

Wine match
A summery rosé

4 tablespoons extra virgin olive oil
4 red capsicums, cored, seeded and
    sliced into strips
few sprigs thyme
salt and freshly ground black pepper
2 large ripe tomatoes, coarsely chopped
handful of fresh basil leaves, torn
6 small fillets snapper (700g to 1kg in
    total), skin on
2 teaspoons ras el hanout (a spice blend;
    if unavailable use smoked sweet
    paprika)
4 tablespoons extra virgin olive oil
1 lemon, cut into wedges or slices

Heat the oil in a large frying pan, then add the capsicums and thyme. Fry gently over a low heat for about 20 minutes, tossing often so they cook evenly. When the capsicums are soft and almost melting, season with salt and pepper to taste. Transfer to a serving dish. Scatter the tomatoes and basil over the capsicums. Set aside.

Rub the flesh side of the fish fillets with the spice and salt and pepper. Heat the second measure of oil in a frying pan until almost smoking. Reduce the heat to low and place the fish in the pan, spice side down, for 3 minutes. Turn over and cook the skin side for a further 3–4 minutes (the cooking time depends on the thickness of the fillets).

Serve the fish immediately with lemon wedges and the capsicums.

HARVEST BAKED CHICKEN

I first made this dish for a *Cuisine* feature celebrating the harvest, which we photographed on the terrace of the well-sited Takatu Lodge. It has been one of the most-loved recipes I have ever created. Citrus grows plentifully in the Omaha Flats area, so there are always lots of lemons year round for drinks or for using in deliciously easy recipes such as this.

Serves 8–10

Wine match
Chardonnay

1 organic chicken, cut into large portions (or 4 legs cut into drumsticks and thighs)
½ cup black olives
½ cup green olives
3 tablespoons diced preserved lemon peel
2 juicy lemons, cut into wedges
½ cup rosemary leaves
sea salt and freshly ground black pepper
4 tablespoons extra virgin olive oil
2 tablespoons good-quality balsamic vinegar
15–20 cherry tomatoes
chopped parsley to garnish

Preheat the oven to 200°C. Place the chicken portions in a large roasting dish. Toss with the olives, preserved lemon, lemon wedges, rosemary leaves, salt and pepper, olive oil and balsamic until well mixed.

Place in the oven and roast for 25 minutes, turning occasionally. Add the tomatoes and continue to roast for another 20 minutes. Check to ensure the thighs are cooked well. Remove from the oven and allow to rest for 10 minutes, then transfer to a large serving platter.

Serve hot or at room temperature, sprinkled with parsley.

GRILLED LAMB WITH AN ASIAN-STYLE MARINADE

After I have been to the market I love to go to Stubbs Village Butchery where there is an incredible array of condiments. If I am having friends over for dinner my favourite purchase is a boned leg of lamb, which I marinate with herbs from John and Wiwan Hay's stall. They grow a wonderful selection of Asian herbs and vegetables in their Pak Thai garden. It's so easy to throw this spicy lamb on the barbecue to grill and it's always popular with guests.

Serves 6–8

Wine match
A rich shiraz

1 boned and butterflied leg of lamb
3 tablespoons soy sauce
1 tablespoon sesame oil
3 tablespoons vegetable oil
2 teaspoons salt
1 tablespoon cumin
3 kaffir lime leaves, finely chopped
1 cup Vietnamese mint leaves, chopped
1 small red chilli, seeded and finely sliced
3 limes
1 cup fresh coriander leaves

Place the lamb in a large pan. Combine the soy sauce, sesame oil, vegetable oil, salt, cumin, lime leaves, mint, chilli and the juice and grated zest of 2 limes in a bowl and mix well. Pour this mixture over the lamb, turning to coat completely. Cover with plastic wrap or tinfoil and set aside for at least 1 hour (or refrigerate overnight).

(Return the lamb to room temperature if it has been refrigerated). Place on a heated barbecue, preferably one with a lid. Keep the burners alight on either side of the meat, but do not put the lamb over direct heat — if the fat drips onto the flames below, the flares-ups could burn the meat.

Close the lid and cook for 40–50 minutes, turning after 25 minutes, for juicy, slightly rare meat. Check occasionally to ensure the meat is cooking evenly. When it has reached the desired degree of doneness, cover with tinfoil and set aside in a warm place to rest and allow the juices to set.

To serve, carve into thin slices and garnish with the coriander leaves and wedges of the remaining lime.

DUCK LEG CASSEROLE

At the Matakana farmers' market, Peter Mitchell of Hill Foot Farm presents a real feast of his Mahurangi duck treats — from eggs to an authentic Chinese-style Peking duck, ready cooked to take home. I love to make a casserole with the portions of duck legs. This dish may seem time-consuming, but after the initial 15 minutes it takes to prepare it for the oven, the casserole will take care of itself and all you need to go with it is a plate of freshly steamed beans, preferably snowbeans.

Serves 4

Wine match
Pinot noir

4 duck leg and thigh portions
3 tablespoons flour
salt and freshly ground black pepper
4 tablespoons extra virgin olive oil
4 shallots, finely chopped
4 medium kumara, peeled and cut into
   5cm pieces
12–15 pitted prunes
2 bay leaves
2 cups red wine
1 cup chicken stock
5–6 sprigs fresh thyme
½ cup chopped parsley

Trim a little of the fat from the duck portions. Dust the duck with flour seasoned with salt and pepper.

Heat the olive oil in a heavy frying pan and brown the duck well all over. Transfer to a heavy stove- and ovenproof casserole dish.

Preheat the oven to 190°C.

Pour off some of the fat from the pan, leaving about 4 tablespoons. Add the shallots to the pan and fry gently for 4–5 minutes until golden, then add the kumara, prunes and bay leaves, and toss together well over the heat. Add the red wine, stock and thyme and bring to a fast simmer for about 5 minutes. Pour this mixture over the duck, return the casserole to the heat and bring to a simmer again.

Cover the casserole, place in the oven and bake for about 30 minutes, checking to ensure the liquid does not dry up. Season well, allow to rest for about 10 minutes, then serve scattered with chopped parsley and accompanied by steamed beans.

STEAK SANDWICHES WITH ONIONS, GREENS AND HERB MAYONNAISE

The excellent Matakana Patisserie has beautiful freshly baked ciabatta every day. But on weekends I look for their famous sourdough boule. Sliced and toasted, it is the perfect vehicle for a steak sandwich, which is the best lunch I can think of. I get the guys at Stubbs Village Butchery to cut thick pieces of sirloin, which I barbecue, then slice. For a final touch I top the sandwiches with a delicious chutney from the farmers' market made by Lorraine North of Windfall Foods.

Makes 4

Wine match
A cabernet blend

1 red onion, peeled and sliced
4 tablespoons extra virgin olive oil
8 slices sourdough bread
2 slices very thickly cut sirloin steak
homemade mayonnaise
4 crisp lettuce leaves
4 slices beefsteak tomato
salt and freshly ground black pepper
4 tablespoons chutney

Place the onions in a heavy frying pan with 2 tablespoons of the oil. Fry gently until they are soft and starting to darken and caramelise. Remove from the pan and keep warm.

Toast the sourdough and keep warm in a heated oven.

Place the pan over a high heat and add the remaining olive oil. Fry the steaks on each side for about 4 minutes until slightly rare (ensure you don't overcook them) or grill them on the barbecue. Remove from the pan and slice each steak.

Spread mayonnaise on four of the slices of sourdough toast, place a lettuce leaf on each, then a sliced steak. Top each with a slice of tomato and 1 tablespoon of onions. Season with plenty of salt and pepper.

Spread 1 tablespoon of your favourite chutney on each of the remaining four slices of toast; these are the lids to finish the sandwiches. Eat at once.

FRESH BEAN SALAD WITH BABY BEETROOT, RADISHES AND PARSLEY

We're spoilt for choice year round with beans in the Matakana area as they seem to thrive here. Mr Bean, an honesty-stall on the Omaha Flats, has supplied me with beans for years, Quail Farm has lovely scarlet runners throughout the season and recently Andrew Steens at Matakana Fresh has been growing snowbeans, fardenlosas, purple beans and runner beans. Use as many different beans as you can find in this summer salad to serve with fish or at a barbecue.

Serves 6

Wine match
Sauvignon blanc

400g runner beans
400g snowbeans
400g purple beans
2 teaspoons Dijon mustard
2 tablespoons verjuice
4 tablespoons extra virgin olive oil
salt and freshly ground black pepper
6–8 baby beetroot, boiled until tender then peeled
3 radishes, topped and cut into julienne strips
1 small bunch flat-leafed parsley (stalks discarded)

Trim the stalk ends from the beans. If the beans are very long, halve them. The snowbeans can be cut lengthwise into long strips.

Drop the beans into a large saucepan of well-salted boiling water and simmer for 2–3 minutes until they start to soften, but remain green. Immediately drain the beans and place in a bowl of ice-cold water to preserve the bright-green colour.

To make the dressing, shake the mustard, verjuice, oil, salt and pepper together in a small screwtop jar.

Spread the beans over a flat serving platter. Scatter the beetroot and radish julienne over the beans, lightly drizzle the dressing over and top with the parsley leaves. This salad should be served within an hour of dressing or the beans will lose their colour.

FRESH TOMATO SALAD WITH LEMON AND BASIL

During the summer I can find plenty of sweet, ripe outdoor-grown tomatoes in the Matakana farmers' market and at vegetable stands in the district. I love to use Andrew Steens' Matakana Fresh heirloom varieties and tiny baby tomatoes in a salad, dressed with lemon zest, basil and olive oil. There's no need to use any vinegar or lemon juice as tomatoes have plenty of natural acidity. Perfect with a fruity riesling.

Serves 8

Wine match
Riesling

2kg mixed ripe tomatoes (such as large beefsteak tomatoes; yellow, orange or red cherry tomatoes; heirloom varieties and Roma)
1 red onion, sliced paper thin
grated zest of 1 lemon
salt and freshly ground black pepper
pinch of sugar
4 tablespoons light but fruity extra virgin olive oil
handful of basil leaves, torn

Wash and dry the tomatoes, then cut into pieces or slice. Arrange on a large flat platter (don't pile them on top of each other or they can become 'clammy').

Sprinkle the red onion and lemon zest over the tomatoes and season with plenty of salt and pepper and a little sugar. Drizzle with olive oil and scatter the basil over.

PERFECT GREEN SALAD WITH AVOCADOS AND A LIME DRESSING

One of the joys of shopping at the Matakana farmers' market is the array of fresh greens I can get for my salads. Many of the farmers grow delicious lettuce. Jeni Quayle makes lovely salad bags of specially selected greens, edible flowers and herbs from her gardens, and Maria Cobb grows the best mesclun I have ever had. My favourite combination is cos lettuce leaves and rocket tossed with nuggets of creamy avocado, dressed with lime juice and avocado oil.

Serves 6–8

Wine match
Pinot gris

1 head cos lettuce, leaves separated
2–3 handfuls rocket, stalks discarded
1–2 large avocados, peeled and cut
    into chunks
½ cup mint leaves
6 tablespoons avocado oil
juice of 2 limes
1 teaspoon Dijon mustard
sea salt and freshly ground black pepper

Wash the lettuce leaves and rocket and spin in a salad spinner to remove all the water (or dry the leaves with a tea towel). Place in a serving bowl with the avocado and mint leaves.

At this point you can cover the bowl with plastic wrap and refrigerate until needed. This will prevent the greens wilting (but bury the avocado in the greens so it doesn't brown).

To make the dressing, shake the remaining ingredients together in a small screwtop jar.

Immediately before serving, toss the salad well with enough dressing to coat the leaves (but do not drown them — excess dressing will keep in the refrigerator). Serve at once.

POTATOES WITH LEMON, ROSEMARY AND BUTTER

This very simple potato dish is always a hit when served accompanying barbecued lamb or beef. I love the aroma of lemons and rosemary together and, although this is buttery, it is very delicious and an absolute favourite of ours throughout the year.

Serves 6–8

Wine match
Chardonnay

100g butter, melted
1.5kg Agria potatoes, peeled and cut
    into wedges
grated zest of 1 lemon
3–4 rosemary sprigs, leaves stripped
    from stalks and chopped
salt and freshly ground black pepper
1 cup chicken stock

Preheat the oven to 200°C. Use a little of the butter to grease an ovenproof dish.

Arrange the potato wedges in the dish and pour the melted butter over. Grate the lemon zest directly onto the potatoes, then sprinkle the rosemary, salt and pepper over. Heat the chicken stock and pour carefully into the dish around the edges so all the delicious seasonings remain on the potatoes.

Bake for about 1 hour until the potatoes are golden and crisp and the chicken stock has been thoroughly absorbed. Serve at once.

SPICY CARROTS, COURGETTES AND BEANS WITH CORIANDER

I can always be sure of finding fresh coriander at the Matakana farmers' market, and it is a great herb to use to flavour a spicy vegetable mix like this. There are several growers of beans around the Omaha Flats, so throughout the summer there are always fresh beans for dinner. This dish makes a great accompaniment to chicken or fish.

Serves 4–6

Wine match
Riesling

2 tablespoons extra virgin olive oil
small pinch of ground coriander
1 teaspoon cumin seeds
24 baby carrots (350g), well scrubbed
½ cup chicken stock
salt and freshly ground black pepper
3 courgettes, sliced diagonally
2 large handfuls fresh runner beans
   (350g), sliced
3–4 tablespoons chopped fresh coriander

Heat the olive oil in a heavy saucepan and add the ground coriander and the cumin seeds. Fry for about 15 seconds, then add the carrots. Toss well over the heat, then add the chicken stock, and season with salt and pepper. Simmer for 8–10 minutes, then add the courgettes and beans.

Simmer a further 3–4 minutes, then drain, place in a serving dish and scatter with the chopped coriander.

SUMMER TART WITH BLUEBERRIES, STRAWBERRIES AND PEACHES

I always return from the market with a new cooking idea, inspired by the fabulous fresh farm produce. Summer fruits make lovely desserts and I have used them to create this sweet version of the savoury tarts I often make at my beach house. I can't resist the Omaha blueberries and combine them with fresh peaches and strawberries from the market. This easy-to-make tart can be prepared ahead, refrigerated and cooked while the main course is served.

Serves 8

400g puff pastry
1 organic free-range egg, beaten
5 tablespoons demerara sugar
1 teaspoon cinnamon
12–16 strawberries, hulled and halved
6–10 fresh peaches, halved and stones removed
200g blueberries
cream or greek yogurt, to serve

Roll out the puff pastry to fit a loose-bottomed 30cm tart tin. Set aside to rest in a cool place for at least 30 minutes.

Preheat the oven to 200°C.

Brush the pastry with the egg, then sprinkle with the sugar and cinnamon. Place the strawberries and peaches cut side down on the pastry. Scatter the blueberries over, then place the tart in the oven. Turn the heat up to 210°C after the oven door is shut. Bake for 15–20 minutes until the pastry is puffed and golden.

Remove from the oven and allow to cool slightly. Carefully remove the skin from the peaches, as it will be crinkled and scorched. Cut the tart into generous wedges and serve with whipped cream, thick Greek yoghurt or a combination of both.

WINTER FRUIT SALAD WITH HONEY

As the season turns and trees start showing their autumn colours, a whole range of different fruits appear at the roadside stands around Matakana and in the farmers' market. I love the winter fruits that seem almost exotic, like the tamarillos and feijoas I've used in this fresh fruit salad. I believe these fruit need to be poached in a light syrup to bring out the best of their flavour and I love to use the fragrant manuka honey I buy in the market for this.

Serves 6

¼ cup honey
2 cups water
1 teaspoon ground cinnamon
6 feijoas, peeled and halved
6 tamarillos
6 mandarins
3 ripe persimmons
cream or mascarpone, to serve

In a medium saucepan, dissolve the honey in the water with the cinnamon and bring to a gentle simmer. Add the feijoas and poach in the barely simmering liquid for about 5 minutes, until tender. Remove from the liquid and set aside to cool. Reserve the liquid.

Peel the tamarillos, leaving the stalks on, and cut through lengthwise almost to the stalk. Poach gently in the reserved feijoa cooking liquid. This should also take about 5 minutes. Remove from the heat and allow the tamarillos to cool in the liquid.

Peel the mandarins, removing the pith and core. Break into segments.

Peel the persimmons and remove the tops. Cut into neat slices 2–3 cm thick.

Place all the fruit in a glass serving bowl. Boil the poaching syrup until reduced to about 1 cup. Pour this over the fruit and serve warm or cold with sweetened whipped cream or mascarpone sweetened with honey.

BLUEBERRY AND WHITE CHOCOLATE CROISSANT PUDDING

Excellent croissants can be found at the Matakana farmers' market and at the Matakana Patisserie. I love to make a bread and butter pudding with these flaky pastries as it is light and delicious. Blueberries from Rob and Shannon Auton's Omaha blueberry farm are really the star of this dish, but you could also make it with strawberries or raspberries.

Serves 6–8

4 croissants
4 tablespoons butter
200g blueberries (fresh or free-flow frozen)
100g white chocolate, chopped
6 fresh free-range eggs
3 tablespoons sugar
pinch of ground cinnamon
600ml whole milk
icing sugar for dusting
cream, to serve

Butter a large ovenproof baking dish. Preheat the oven to 170°C.

Slice the croissants thickly lengthwise (4–5 slices each). Butter each slice on one side, then place in the dish, overlapping slightly.

Scatter the blueberries and chocolate evenly over the croissant slices.

In a bowl, beat the eggs well with the sugar and cinnamon, then add the milk and beat again.

Carefully pour this batter over the croissants. Push the croissants down so they are thoroughly soaked.

Bake for 30 minutes or until the pudding is golden and puffed on the top. Dredge with sifted icing sugar and serve with cream.

69

MANDARINS IN CARAMEL WITH FRESH YOGHURT

Almost every property in the fertile Omaha Flats area has a variety of citrus trees and by far the largest crop grown commercially is mandarins. With their easy-peeling skins, they are my favourite snack and I crave the refreshing hit of sweet juice you get biting into the segments. This simple dish is a great example of how uncomplicated recipes can be the best, as it has only three ingredients: mandarins, water and sugar.

Serves 6

12 mandarins
1 cup sugar
1 cup hot water
Greek yoghurt, to serve

Peel the mandarins carefully, removing as much of the pith and fibre as you can. Cut each mandarin in half horizontally, then place cut side up in a glass bowl.

To make the caramel, put the sugar in a heavy-based saucepan with ½ cup of the hot water. Place over low heat until the sugar dissolves completely, then increase the heat to medium and bring the sugar and water to a steady boil.
After about 5 minutes most of the

water will have evaporated and the bubbles will become larger. It is important to keep a constant watch. As the sugar mixture begins to turn golden at the edges, swirl the pan around so it cooks evenly.

When the sugar caramelises and turns the colour of golden syrup, remove the pan from the heat and add the remaining hot water, taking care not to splash about any of the caramel as it is dangerously hot. If any lumps form, return the pan to a gentle heat and stir. As the caramel starts to cool, pour it over the mandarins. Keep in a cool place. Serve with thick Greek yoghurt.

RHUBARB AND APPLE CRUMBLE

There always seems to be plenty of rhubarb at the Matakana farmers' market. Its tart flavour is a perfect base for warming puddings; here it is cooked with apple slices and fruity jam for a delicious fruit crumble.

Serves 6

5 stalks fresh rhubarb, chopped
4 apples, peeled, cored and sliced
2–3 tablespoons raspberry or other red fruit jam
2 tablespoons water
1 tablespoon butter
3 tablespoons Calvados
100g cold butter, diced
200g flour
pinch of ground ginger
75g soft brown sugar
whipped cream, to serve

Preheat the oven to 180°C.

Place the rhubarb and apples in a saucepan with the jam and water. Over a low heat, bring to a gentle simmer and cook slowly for about 2 minutes. Take from the heat and stir in the butter and Calvados. Tip this mixture into a buttered baking dish.

To make the crumble, put the remaining indgredients in a bowl. Rub the butter into the flour and sugar with your fingers until the mixture resembles coarse breadcrumbs.

Cover the top of the fruit with the crumble mixture, pressing down slightly so it compacts.

Bake for 25–30 minutes until the top is golden and crunchy. Serve with whipped cream.

The abundance of rich soil on the Omaha Flats and in the Matakana district has meant this region has always been a premium growing area. With the advent of the Matakana farmers' market, and the wineries and olive growers, there has been a huge rise in the number of artisan producers in the surrounding area and some fabulous food can be found to enjoy with the local wines.

There are many more noteworthy people than it is possible to profile on these pages, but the stories that follow are representative of the talent, innovation and hard work seen in the Matakana region.

CHRISTINE AND RICHARD DIDSBURY

Brick Bay

WITHOUT THE VISION and leadership of this talented couple, Matakana would not have the Village, the farmers' market or the outstanding Brick Bay Sculpture Trail. More than 20 years ago the Didsburys bought a coastal farm and for many years spent weekends there with their two daughters, sleeping in a caravan overlooking Kawau Bay. Over time they built a home, established their vineyard, planted orchards and gardens and generally beautified the property.

As they spent more time there, Richard, a developer, saw the potential of the region and bought the timber yard at Matakana with a view to creating a farmers' market, retail centre and boutique cinemas. Architect Noel Lane, who designed their home, was employed for the concept and design and, with local landscapers Garth and Linda Falconer, created a stunning complex that is now the envy of many small New Zealand communities.

The Didsburys have always had a serious interest in art, and both daughters, Anna and Margot, studied at the Elam School of Fine Arts at the University of Auckland. Their love of sculpture and belief in New Zealand artists is expressed by the many important pieces in the Sculpture Trail on their Brick Bay property, in their home and around Matakana Village.

ROB AND SHANNON AUTON

Omaha Blueberries

YOU CAN'T MISS BLUE, the gourmet ice-cream café right on the Matakana roundabout. It is the successful brainchild of talented business pair Rob and Shannon Auton, who gave up their corporate lifestyles and re-established themselves at Omaha as organic blueberry growers when the arrival of their triplets turned their world upside down.

The pair soon realised the importance of adding value to their product by free-flow freezing the berries, creating a delicious blueberry, apple and ginger drink and making blueberry sorbets and ice-creams. Marketing played a large part in their success, and their organic Omaha Blueberries have found their way into niche markets in the United States and Asia.

From the very early days, the Autons made blueberry ice-cream and sorbet from the extensive plantings of organic blueberries on their property, selling their wares directly from the packing shed. Throughout the summer locals in the know would drive up to enjoy an ice-cream under the shade of umbrellas in the orchard and buy freshly picked blueberries to take home. The Autons were also among the first to have a stand at the farmers' market, where their ice-creams and berries proved so popular Shannon opened her café.

GREG SCOPAS

Salumeria Fontana

I FIRST SPOTTED Greg Scopas at the inaugural Food Show in Auckland some years ago. He was offering tastings of his Italian-style cured meat and sausages, and I was really impressed with his products. He had opened a processing factory in West Auckland and was intent on using only organically produced meat. His inspiration came from his father's Italian heritage.

When the Matakana farmers' market opened, Greg was one of the inaugural stallholders. He and his wife Kathryn Katavich fell in love with the area, purchased a rural property north of Warkworth and moved the family there. They also relocated the sausage-manufacturing plant and added their own extra virgin olive oil to the Salumeria Fontana range, as their new property had an olive grove. An olive press came as part of the sale, so Greg presses the oil himself.

Their quality products can be tasted and bought each Saturday at the market, including one of the most popular items ready to eat: hot Sicilian-style sweet fennel sausages, served on fresh bread rolls with rocket and sweet chilli sauce.

ANDREW STEENS

Matakana Fresh

ANDREW STEENS is known in the Matakana region for cultivating bromeliads and heliconias at his property on the Warkworth to Matakana road. He recently moved to Point Wells, where he is also growing heirloom tomatoes, special varieties of beans and other unusual vegetables in season.

Andrew has come almost full circle, as he started out in horticulture when he left school. He worked in Mt Maunganui for many years, first growing vegetables, then kiwifruit and after that cut flowers. For many years he concentrated on his bromeliads and heliconias, as well as writing two books on the former, but is now enjoying working with vegetables as well. He says that with so many interesting varieties available, it is hard to know what to grow.

Andrew's produce can be found in the Matakana farmers' market most Saturdays throughout summer.

TONY GIBBS

Ezypeel Mandarins

FOR MOST OF the week, Tony Gibbs works at his high-flying corporate day job, but when at home on the rich, fertile soils of Omaha Flats, he and his wife Val oversee one of the country's largest citrus orchards.

Their 57 hectares of seedless satsuma mandarin trees are carefully tended sheltered by high casuarinas and pine hedges, clipped with almost military precision. The effect is like a series of enormous rooms and Tony runs the orchard as if it were a well-groomed park.

A constant round of pruning, thinning and harvesting produces more than 1000 tonnes of mandarins annually. That's an astounding 13 million pieces of fruit each year that are sent to Mangere for washing, waxing and labelling with Tony's Ezypeel sticker. The mandarins are mostly destined for supermarkets and stores around New Zealand but a few tonnes are exported to Japan.

LYNETTE DUNN AND TREVOR SMITH

Orata Marine
Farms

WHEN LYNETTE DUNN and Trevor Smith first brought their oysters to the Matakana farmers' market they rotated each week with other oyster farmers from the Mahurangi Harbour. The group felt it was important that visitors to the market realised oysters were farmed in the Matakana area. Three years on, most of the others in the group have dropped out, but Lynette is there every week with bags of live local oysters. Most of the oysters from their Orata Marine Farms are exported by seafood wholesalers in Auckland.

Trevor started out in aquaculture when he left school aged 15 and, from his initial foray working for a marron grower, he has built a business and now owns four oyster leases. The Mahurangi Harbour, which has a number of oyster leases, is rich in oyster spat, so technically these are wild oysters. Trevor harvests them when they have grown for around 14 months. Many people do not realise oysters are seasonal. They are best, in Trevor's opinion, from May through to mid-January, when they are plump and juicy. Every oyster is a different shape, and this quirkiness comes with the high-quality wild catch. However, between mid-January and April there is still a market for oysters, mostly overseas in the French islands of the Pacific where the people enjoy the skinny, more even shape of the New Zealand summer harvest.

MAREE CLAYDON

Quail Farm Fresh
Vegetables

A BOARD DISPLAYING the current produce from Maree Claydon's gardens at Quail Farm can be spotted on the road out to Omaha Beach. Maree was raised on a farm in the area and developed an appreciation of the high quality of the land on Omaha Flats, proven to be some of the best soil in Rodney district.

She always dreamed of growing vegetables there in the latter part of her life, but the ideal block of land came up far sooner than Maree imagined. While husband Paul commutes to his development job in Auckland, Maree cultivates an extensive garden on her dream plot in partnership with her father.

Her customer base has burgeoned and she's kept busy year round, with regulars not just from the neighbouring area, but also customers who drive from Auckland to buy her exceptional fruits and freshly harvested vegetables. Her crops include potatoes, capsicums, beans, tomatoes, beets and lettuces, along with fruit from her citrus orchard, all displayed at her honesty-box stand. Also look for preserves and jams from both Maree's and her mother's kitchens.

91

LORRAINE NORTH

Windfall Foods

WHEN LORRAINE NORTH moved from her pocket-handkerchief garden in Ponsonby to a rambling Matakana property that has been an orchard since 1905, she wondered what she'd do with all the fruit. A local vegetable store suggested she could make some jam that one of their customers had been searching for, and that sparked the business that Windfall Foods has become.

Lorraine carries her numerous jars and bottles, filled with every conceivable type of jam, jelly and preserve, to the Matakana farmers' market each week. She gathers organic vegetables and fruits from around the district, then cooks her preserves and fills her jars in the bowling club kitchen at Snells Beach.

Her biggest-selling item is the kasundi, a spicy condiment that goes perfectly with grilled meats. Customers also like her old-fashioned jellies and jams such as crab apple and quince, and Lorraine's lemon, lime and passionfruit curds. Selected lines can also be found in local stores.

LYNNE CURRY

Brookview
Teahouse

LYNNE CURRY HAS had a lifelong fascination with food and a passion for gardening, and the two have come together beautifully at her classy eatery in Matakana, the Brookview Teahouse. Walk in and sniff the aroma of fresh baking from Lynne's open kitchen and be tempted by delicate pastries and cakes. This is the first business venture for Lynne, who always dreamed of owning her own delicatessen.

Lynne and her partner Pete Mullins bought a large block of land in Matakana, but just when they were ready to build their home, Pete was seconded to Sydney. On their return, Matakana Village was taking shape and Christine Didsbury persuaded Lynne to shift her sights from the deli idea to a tearoom in the old cottage over the road. Thinking it would be an easy option, Lynne agreed, and her food, cooked from scratch with love every day, has quickly become the favourite of locals seeking delicious seasonal fresh delights.

The raised gardens in the grounds, planted with herbs, vegetables and a few ornamental plants, supply the kitchen. It's Lynne's dream to be able to devote her menu entirely to this produce, year round. Seasonal food is her focus and, even though she cooks every day, she and her staff never tire of discussing new ideas and twists on traditional fare. It's not quite the easy job she had imagined, but Lynne loves the contact with her customers and maintains her fascination and love affair with food.

LINDESAY SMITH AND ANGELA STECHMAN

Matakana Coffee Roasters

LINDESAY SMITH HAS always had an eye for the main coffee chance. In 1989 he opened Sierra Café on Jervois Rd, Herne Bay, in Auckland, the first of what has become a franchise chain. He went on to set up nine more Sierras, before leaving New Zealand to start a Sierra café/restaurant in Noosa, Queensland.

Then in 2003 he and his partner Angela Stechman moved to the Matakana area, as they wanted to be part of a growers' and producers' community. Not long after that they became the coffee operators at the farmers' market when it opened and almost every Saturday since, there have been lengthy queues for their smart coffee service and delicious croque monsieurs.

They expanded their business by opening the Black Dog Coffee and Country Kitchen over the road from the market, selling that business 14 months later when their child was born. They have continued to operate their Matakana Coffee Roasters business, producing the Matakana Coffee brand and recently adding a second, Love Shack, a Fair Trade organic coffee blend. They operate their roastery from a small 'shack' to the rear of the market above the river, and their irregular opening hours are signalled by a flag which they hoist when they are there. Local coffee lovers spot it immediately and pop by for a superb cup of the latest brew.

MATAKANA OLIVE CO-OPERATIVE

THE MATAKANA DISTRICT has proven to be an ideal environment for growing olives. Many locals with lifestyle blocks and small farms have planted olive trees that range through all the varietals suitable for making olive oil. Seventeen of these growers have formed the Matakana Olive Co-operative and produce fine extra virgin olive oil that is pressed and marketed locally.

Their oils, currently produced in two blends, have won medals in every competition they have entered to date. Pressed at a large purpose-built facility in the Whangaripo Valley, the oil is sold at the Matakana farmers' market each week, with the various cooperative members taking turns to offer tastings and sales.

Every batch is certified by Olives New Zealand and carries the red dot sticker which guarantees the oil is extra virgin and produced from only New Zealand olives.

JOE POLAISCHER AND TRISH ALLEN

Rainbow Valley
Farm

THE EARLIEST SUPPORTERS of the farmers' market concept were Joe Polaischer and Trish Allen, owners of Rainbow Valley Farm. It was Joe's photos of a market he had visited in Japan that became the inspiration for the market structure,and his philosophy of sustainable, organic agriculture has been a continuing inspiration in the community.

Rainbow Valley Farm, often staffed by WWOOFers (Willing Workers On Organic Farms), is a sustainable farm operated and managed by the principles of permaculture. Anyone who buys the innovative and original produce from the farm's stand at the market is in for a taste treat of goodness.

Sadly Joe died suddenly in early 2008, but his work is continued on the farm, with Trish at the helm and a bevy of helpers who continue to come from around the world to spend time in the district and work in the gardens.

TYRONE VINCENT

Matakana
Patisserie

TYRONE AND DELWYN VINCENT had been looking for an opportunity to move out of Auckland in 2001 when they learned of a rundown bakery in Matakana. They bought it, closed it for five weeks and reopened as the Pop In Patisserie, one of the first of the new wave of businesses that helped to put Matakana on the modern map.

Tyrone is a talented, passionate baker, and his range of sourdough breads and fancy pies became famous overnight — so greatly admired that there were seemingly endless queues of customers stretching out the door and down the street.

Five years later they moved further up Matakana Valley Rd to a new, larger building and a special stand-alone bakery factory a few doors away. Rebranding the business as Matakana Patisserie, they offered three times the range of baked goods and speciality patisserie, created space for guests to sit and have their coffee and food, increased their staff from the original three to 35 — and they've never looked back.

Delwyn guides the retail shop (their second shop opens in Mangawhai in late 2008) and oversees all the administrative details. And the queues are now in the shop rather than out the door.

JAMES AND REBECCA McCARTHY

Stubbs Village Butchery

THE STYLISH STUBBS Village Butchery has fast become the heart of Matakana Village. Walk in and you'll be assailed by tempting aromas created in the demonstration kitchen by the resident chef, while a DVD screen high on the wall will be showing the latest Jamie Oliver or Rick Stein programme.

Owners James and Rebecca McCarthy took over a traditional butcher shop in Warkworth in 2005 and turned it around by making it into a haven for food lovers. They have now expanded their business and opened a second store in Matakana, which is crammed with a wide variety of high-quality meat, poultry, fish and deli meats. The free-standing shelves are stocked with every gourmet item a cook could want.

James is dedicated to sourcing the best produce New Zealand offers and believes it's important to ensure the traceability of food products. He stocks free-range and organic items wherever possible. And for those seeking new menu ideas, cooking classes are held regularly.

PETE CLEMENTSON

Matakana
Smokehouse

WHEN PETE CLEMENTSON felt the desire to walk away from his corporate city life, Matakana was where he and his wife Kim decided they would head. They'd had a caravan at nearby Martins Bay, loved the idea of fishing and were determined to leave Auckland. The pair identified the niche for a smokehouse in the Matakana district. Pete is from the South Island and whenever he holidayed in Motueka, the famous Smokehouse at Mapua was always his first port of call.

He has set up a large smoker in a small green shed near the centre of the township. Each week does two or three cold smokes of salmon, fish, oysters, vegetables and pork fillets, and he intends to increase production to keep up with demand. The cold-smoking process imports a deliciously moist, smoky flavour to the food, which is all of the highest quality.

Matakana Smokehouse products can be found at the farmers' market each week and also by direct sale from the smokehouse when Pete is there.

BARBARA SOUTER

Market Providores

AS THE INAUGURAL manager of the Matakana farmers' market, Barbara Souter fell in love with the wonderful produce that the farmers and small producers brought along. For about three years she was at the market every Saturday, arriving as early as 6.30am to supervise stallholders and assist where needed. In her managerial role she was an integral part of the market's success and also ran her own stand, selling bags (and umbrellas on wet days) to visitors laden with produce they could not resist.

Barbara also attended the annual Farmers' Market New Zealand conferences, coming into contact with artisan producers from around the country. So when it was time to move on from her position she found a shop in Snells Beach and opened Market Providores. She stocks it with fine artisan products and delicacies from throughout New Zealand, most of which first appeared in farmers' markets. Hot soup, sandwiches, ready-made meals and coffee are also offered, as are many hard-to-find ingredients for the pantry.

JENI QUAYLE

Waybyond
Organics

PASSIONATE ABOUT FRESH organically grown produce, Jeni Quayle often works late into the night on Fridays, preparing bags of mixed leaves, flowers and vegetables for the salad mixes she sells at the farmers' market. She has a wonderful organic farm near Wellsford, to the north of Matakana, but is totally dedicated to her regular customers who make a beeline each Saturday morning for her special eggs, salads and a host of other seasonal vegetables and fruits straight from her farm.

Her flock of poultry includes Araucana hens, originally from South America. These blue-feathered birds surprisingly lay blue-shelled eggs. A mixed carton of Waybyond eggs is a cook's delight, as the yolks are the brightest shade of golden yellow — proof that the hens roam free. Jeni's partner, Greg Fletcher, can often be seen busking at the market entrance.

JON AND MORAG STANDBROOK

Mustardmakers

EVERY SATURDAY JON STANDBROOK is at the farmers' market, selling his range of innovative and tasty mustards, marmalades and chutneys. With his wife Morag, he constructed a tiny shop and production kitchen, Mustardmakers at the Plantery, in Puhoi. Their business has been a success story, as in four years they have built up a customer base, exporting to Hong Kong and Singapore and supplying many specialty stores throughout New Zealand.

They first used their land to raise edible plants for sale at the gate, but their fascination for mustard led them into food production. They make a range of nine mustards (the top sellers are those made with New Zealand native herbs and honeys), organic chutneys, dips and rubs.

SILVANA SILVESTRO

Silvana's Gourmet
Italian Food

A RELATIVE NEWCOMER to the farmers' market, Silvana Silvestro has quietly won the hearts of food lovers in the district with the stunning array of pasta dishes she prepares from home in her certified commercial kitchen. This is the food Silvana grew up with in her Sicilian family home in Melbourne and she has perfected it on her numerous trips to visit family in Italy.

Rolling her own egg-based pasta is essential to the handmade ravioli and lasagne — which I regard as the most delicious I have tried – filled with aubergine and chopped boiled egg and swathed in a rich homemade tomato ragù. Her crisp cannoli are a treat, oozing with luxurious vanilla custard, and her suppli (deep-fried risotto balls) are light as air with a tangy blue-cheese filling.

Silvana is now working on a range of ready-cooked meals to be sold in stores or in the many B&Bs around Matakana.

JOHN AND WIWAN HAY

Pak Thai

JOHN HAY MET his wife, Wiwan, while working in northern Thailand as a jeweller. Wi is from the area close to Laos and when the pair decided in 1993 to live in New Zealand, they dreamed of a place in the country where they could grow the Thai herbs and vegetables they were used to. Their large plot of land in Matakana is perfect for an Asian garden, as the climate is warm, with the regular rainfall needed for year-round cultivation. There's even a small stream behind their house where the Vietnamese mint thrives.

John and Wi now work full time in their garden, selling their produce at the Matakana farmers' market and in Auckland at the Takapuna market on Sundays. Their stall is filled with Asian herbs and vegetables such as water spinach, bok choy, gai choy, Asian chives, Thai basil, ginger, chillies and kaffir limes and leaves, as well as many more European vegetables freshly harvested from their garden and glasshouses. When she has time, Wi, an excellent cook, prepares Thai specialities and snacks to sell, too.

WINE, VINES
AND MORE

Once known for dairy, sheep and cattle farming, and some horticulture around Omaha, the Matakana area now has a wealth of vineyards and new wine labels that are changing the way it is perceived.

Locals and visitors alike are surprised to observe the extensive plantings of new vines that continually spring up in paddocks and on north-facing slopes about the district. It is a fast-growing wine region, although the wines are mainly produced by small boutique operations and production is small.

The predominant varietals that appear to thrive in the district are pinot gris and flora for white wines and cabernet sauvignon, merlot, cabernet franc and malbec to make Bordeaux-style blended red wines.

To taste almost every wine made in the region head to The Vintry, a well-run wine bar next to the Matakana Cinemas in the heart of the Village.

Visitors to The Vintry can feast on simple tapas platters and explore the many labels and styles. Or you can just have a simple glass of wine (which can also be taken into the cinema).

ASCENSION WINE ESTATE

This Spanish Mission-styled winery on the Warkworth to Matakana road is the pride of owners Darryl and Bridget Soljan. Their popular restaurant offers lunch seven days and dinner Thursday to Saturday. Adjacent is the tasting room and sales centre, the Belfry (a function centre and wedding venue) and a barrel storage hall and winemaking area.

Darryl is a member of the Soljan family of West Auckland, which has been involved in the wine industry since the 1930s, and he has proudly carried their traditions to Matakana. The vineyard's north-facing slopes are well drained and frost free, and Darryl believes the terroir imparts an earthy Bordeaux-like character to his wines.

Ascension makes chardonnay, merlot, viognier, flora and pinotage at Matakana and also has a Marlborough vineyard producing sauvignon blanc and riesling. Several of the wines have attracted top ratings and the Epiphany Matakana Pressings is the flagship wine of the range.

Live music, poetry and gigs are arranged throughout the year. Additionally, petanque, a children's play area including a sandpit, outdoor chess and a huge potager garden make this a premium destination.

**480 Matakana Rd, Matakana,
ph: (09) 422 9601,
www.ascensionwine.co.nz**

BRICK BAY WINES

Christine and Richard Didsbury have brought great vision and style to the region. They have established and developed their Brick Bay coastal farm over the past 20 years and are the prime movers behind the Matakana Village and farmers' market.

Visitors to their Brick Bay winery near Snells Beach can taste the wines made on the property and enjoy platters in the spectacular Glass House tasting room, which is cantilevered over a large pond. Designed by architect Noel Lane, it also serves as a centre for the Brick Bay Sculpture Trust's Sculpture Trail, which winds around the vineyard and through some lovely bush.

Christine completed a winemaking and viticulture course by correspondence before establishing the vineyard on the farm. She had the vision to choose pinot gris before it became the wine that everyone wants to drink today. More than half the plantings are red grapes used in their rosé and a Bordeaux blend, which in the best years is their flagship wine, Pharos.

Recently the Didsburys have been joined on the vineyard by their daughter Anna, an arts graduate, who manages the viticulture and helps oversee the administration of the Sculpture Trail and the tasting room.

Arabella Lane (off Mahurangi East Rd), Snells Beach, ph: (09) 425 4690, www.brickbay.co.nz

HERON'S FLIGHT VINEYARD

David Hoskins and Mary Evans have one of the original vineyards in the area, and although they originally planted cabernet sauvignon and chardonnay, they've now replaced their vines with Italian grapes. They sourced budwood from Tuscany for their sangiovese, their top wine, and their dolcetto is from Piedmont. They also make a second, lighter sangiovese, Il Rosso, along with non-alcoholic grape juice that has no added sugar or preservatives.

Mary is interested in history, is an enthusiastic food lover, and runs the recently constructed villa-style restaurant and tasting room where tables have restful views over the surrounding countryside. The food offered for brunch, lunch and dinner is designed to match Heron's Flight wine.

A private room can be booked for groups. Homemade olive oil, verjuice and a range of preserves and spreads are stocked under Mary's Flights of Fancy label. Culinary gardens on the property are laid out to tell the stories of the people who settled the northern region of New Zealand.

**49 Sharp Rd, Matakana,
ph: (09) 422 7915, www.heronsflight.co.nz**

HYPERION WINES

John and Jill Crone established their tiny vineyard in 1994 with a small north-facing plot on Omaha Flats Rd, next to Providence (see page 140).

They now have several plantings of red grape varietals that include cabernet sauvignon, merlot, pinot noir and malbec. The pair sources white grapes for their pinot gris and chardonnay from another local vineyard that they planted.

Over the years, Hyperion wines have received multiple awards at wine competitions, both locally and on the international stage.

The winery, named after the mythical Greek god of the sun, is in a converted cowshed at the end of Tongue Farm Rd, past the Morris & James pottery. The Crones have used the names of Hyperion's offspring for some of the varietals, including Titan, Gaia, Helios and Kronos.

Hyperion also has a luxury cottage to rent on Whitmore Rd, Matakana, with extensive views over the vineyard and surrounding countryside.

Visitors are welcome to taste on weekends and holidays.

**Tongue Farm Rd, Matakana,
ph: (09) 422 9375,
www.hyperion-wines.co.nz**

OMAHA BAY VINEYARD

Sitting on a prime hilltop site, Omaha Bay Vineyard's restaurant and tasting room have grandstand views over Omaha Bay and out to Little Barrier Island. It's a casual, rustic building, with outdoor seating where guests can enjoy wines and tasting platters of local produce.

Hegman and Beverley Foster changed careers — he was a civil engineer and she was an artist, painter and photographer — to grow grapes, make wine and offer hospitality at their newly constructed winery. Hegman was inspired by his great-grandfather, a Croatian who came to New Zealand as a gumdigger and planted vines in Huapai in 1932 to produce Golden Age port.

Their vineyard is planted with 11,000 vines of pinot gris, syrah, Bordeaux blends and Montepulciano grapes and the wines made for them by freelance winemaker Shane Cox.

**189 Takatu Rd, Matakana,
ph: (09) 423 0022, www.omahabay.co.nz**

RANSOM WINES

Robin and Marion Ransom's winery is found just off the main highway a few kilometres south of Warkworth. The stylish, modern, architect-designed building is home to the winemaking facilities and a welcoming cellar-door operation.

The pair have been dedicated to sustainably producing wine from their estate since the mid-1990s and have a good following in the region and in Auckland. Two Bordeaux blends, two styles of chardonnay, syrah and an unusual vin gris (rosé) are made by Robin from fruit grown on the estate. She also makes limoncello and grappa.

Marion creates carefully considered food platters to match the Ransom wines, and the signature set-lunch platter has a variety of seasonal vegetable dishes, dips and olives with meats, local cheeses and baskets of specialty breads. Lighter platters are also offered, including a cheese platter and a 'sweet treats' platter to accompany dessert wines and coffee.

46 Valerie Close, Warkworth,
ph: (09) 425 8862,
www.ransomwines.co.nz

SALTINGS ESTATE

For a long period, Saltings Estate was better known for boutique accommodation overlooking the inner harbour at Sandspit.

Maureen and Terry Baines produced their first wines in 2006: red wines made by John Worth for their two labels, Saltings Estate and Sandspit Cove. The Baines grow their vines according to biodynamic principles, and their wines are full-bodied and rich in flavour.

The original charming boutique bed-and-breakfast building overlooking the Sandspit inlet is set down a long driveway and surrounded by bush. The three rooms there have en suites, one with a separate lounge facing a private courtyard, and gourmet breakfasts are served family-style in the sunny kitchen.

The Vintner's Haven has been constructed at the end of the vineyard, with two further fully equipped, self-catering apartments with views over the vineyard and estuary.

1210 Sandspit Rd, Warkworth, ph: (09) 425 9670, www.saltings.co.nz

TAKATU VINEYARD AND LODGE

John and Heather Forsman have built an enviable lifestyle: their luxury lodge is situated on a stunning site overlooking their vineyard, with views to Mt Tamahunga and the surrounding lush landscape. John, an Air New Zealand pilot, is passionate about his wines, made by independent winemaker Herb Friedli.

John's philosophy is to grow low-yielding vines tended by hand at every step of vineyard production. Their pinot gris, made in a bone-dry style, has found instant popularity and each vintage has sold out. Their red wines, from merlot, cabernet franc and malbec grapes, were released under the Kawau Bay label when produced from very young vines, but the 2005 vintage is the first to be released under the premium Takatu label. Tastings at the lodge are by appointment only.

The ultra-modern lodge is set among the vines. All four of the large luxury suites, each with a bathroom opening to the outdoors and built of New Zealand native timbers and natural stone, has extensive views over the vineyard. Local wool and cotton fabrics have been used throughout and an organic breakfast is included in the tariff. Dinners can be catered by arrangement. Complimentary wine tasting is offered with antipasto platters to guests.

**518 Whitmore Rd, Matakana,
ph: (09) 423 0299, www.takatuwine.co.nz**

TI POINT VINEYARD

Three generations of women are involved in Ti Point wines. Tracy Haslam makes the wine from this north-facing 20-hectare property, and her mother Jan and grandmother Nan work on what was originally a 'lifestyle' property.

Tracy, a talented winemaker, is married to David Mason of Sacred Hill and works from their home base in Hawke's Bay. She crafts her Ti Point label red wines, which are merlot-predominant blended with cabernet franc, from grapes grown on her mother's vineyard. Ti Point One (a merlot) and Ti Point Two (a merlot-cabernet franc blend), inky dark with smooth, rounded flavours, sell out quickly and her rosé, a full-bodied dry style with fruity aromas, is a perfect summer drink. Viognier,

chardonnay, sauvignon blanc and pinot gris are also bottled under the Ti Point label, made with fruit sourced from Hawke's Bay and Marlborough.

Ti Point Vineyard Retreat, an architecturally designed house perched on a ridge with almost 360-degree views, overlooks Omaha Beach and the Big Omaha estuary. It can be hired as a self-catering private house or as a B&B hosted by Jan. There are horses and donkeys on the farm, and Leigh, Pakiri Beach and Matakana are all within a short drive.

Tairere Rd, Matakana, ph: (09) 422 6908, www.tipoint.co.nz

OTHER WINES TO LOOK FOR IN MATAKANA

THE ANTIPODEAN: Fine 'old world' wine from a single vineyard planted in the 1970s. It is made by Michelle Chignell-Vuletic and is available from selected outlets.

CONTOUR ESTATE: Small family-owned vineyard on Takatu Rd that produces syrah.

THE GABION: A premium Bordeaux-style red made by winemaker Tracy Haslam from grapes grown on a small family estate overlooking Omaha Beach.

HINCHCO FAMILY ESTATE: This small family estate at Monarch Downs makes a classic reserve merlot, a rosé and a dessert merlot. Tastings are offered at Andrea Hinchco's well-stocked store, Taste, at 2 Neville St, Warkworth.

MATAKANA ESTATE: A large winery on the main road from Warkworth to Matakana. Their wine-tasting facility is currently closed.

PROVIDENCE VINEYARD: Jim Vuletic makes premium red wines on this picture-perfect hillside site on the Omaha Flats. His wines, including the flagship merlot, are sought after by international buyers and mostly sold overseas, but occasionally the cellar door opens on holiday weekends for tastings.

GILLMAN ESTATE, COXHEAD CREEK, MERRYFIELDS, MAHURANGI RIVER and **HAWKS NEST** are other labels that have recently been offered in reasonable quantities and are worth checking out.

ART AND INSPIRATION

ART AND INSPIRATION

PREVIOUS PAGE: The Glass House at the Brick Bay Sculpture Trail

OPPOSITE: Virginia King's *Sliver*, 2006, at the Brick Bay Sculpture Trail

The inspirational and interesting landscape, and a wealth of places where artists can hide away to work in solitude and tranquil surroundings, mean it's no surprise that art plays a large part in the culture of the Matakana district.

There are several worthwhile galleries that I love visiting, with premium works of art displayed and for sale. Two important sculpture gardens can be found in the district: both the Brick Bay Sculpture Trail and Zealandia Sculpture Garden are must-sees for art lovers.

Every two years the Tawharanui Regional Park benefits the from the *Art in the Woolshed* exhibition and sale, organised by TOSSI (Tawharanui Open Sanctuary Society Inc) and many of the galleries mount excellent displays and shows from respected local and national artists as part of the event. It's well worth taking the drive to the Regional Park to see the show.

There are also two groups of artists in the area, the Mahurangi Group and the Matakana Valley Rd Group, and their biennial art shows are always a joy.

A FINE LINE GALLERY

One of the most recent additions to the art scene in the area, this art space is found at Charlies Gelato Garden. The gallery showcases a diverse range of art forms including painting, print, ceramics, photography and mixed media. Exhibitions change every four weeks.

The gallery is closed from June to September.

17 Sharp Rd, Matakana,
ph: (09) 422 7942, www.afineline.co.nz

ART IN THE WOOLSHED

This much-anticipated biennial regional art event is held in the woolshed at the Tawharanui Regional Park (opposite), held to raise funds for the Tawharanui Open Sanctuary Society Inc (TOSSI). The volunteer members of TOSSI work alongside the Auckland Regional Council to protect and restore the natural habitat and foster the reinstatement of endangered species within the park. Curated by artist Barry Lett, the exhibition is open to the public and all works are for sale.

Paintings, sculpture, glass and clay works, wooden furniture and other art works are exhibited. The sculpture in the park is particularly interesting to view.

For further information see
www.tossi.org.nz

BRICK BAY SCULPTURE TRAIL

FOLLOWING PAGES:
Brick Bay Sculpture
Trail

This trail showcases works by contemporary New Zealand artists, both emerging and established, including such well-known names as Virginia King, Jeff Thomson, Fatu Feu'u, Peter Lange, Lyndal Jefferies and Gretchen Albrecht.

The sculptures are specifically created new works, selected by a curatorial panel and available for purchase.

The two-kilometre trail wends its way around the Brick Bay vineyard, through pristine native bush and farmland. The track is an easy walk suitable for all ages and takes a leisurely hour to cover.

The Glass House at Brick Bay is the gateway to this trail and is a relaxing place where visitors can browse through art publications over a coffee or glass of wine and platters of local food. Tastings and purchase of Brick Bay wines produced from the grapes in the surrounding vineyards are available.

Arabella Lane (off Mahurangi East Rd), Snells Beach, ph: (09) 425 4690, www.brickbaysculpture.co.nz

DRAGONFLY CAFÉ AND GALLERY

This breezy café and gallery changed owners in late 2008. The new owners are dedicated to producing and displaying art and exhibitions of high quality featuring established and emerging artists, and have employed an experienced art-lover to look after the gallery part of the business. The display space is well designed, with plenty of light and a lovely outlook to the river. An added bonus is the adjacent café with deli-style takeout food suitable for picnics and road trips.

615 Matakana Rd, Matakana,
ph: (09) 422 7330

MATAKANA GALLERY AND DESIGN

This is one of the largest art galleries in the region. On the ground level of the main building at the Matakana Country Park, it also has a large mezzanine floor where exhibitions of painting and photography are frequently mounted.

The gallery displays more than 100 paintings, along with sculpture, jewellery, glass pieces and ceramics. The works are selected from artists in the district and from around New Zealand.

Matakana Country Park,
1 Omaha Flats Rd, Matakana,
ph: (09) 422 9790,
www.matakanacountrypark.co.nz

MATAKANA VALLEY RD ART GROUP

MAHURANGI GROUP

There's something about the tranquillity and isolation of Matakana Valley Rd that has inspired artists to live there. The artists living on the road have formed a casual community art group, getting together irregularly to exchange ideas, support each other and chat about their work. They hold dinners and every two years organise a group show to display and sell their works. Painters Virginia Leonard, Mike Petre, Mark Wooller and Mark Lewington, sculptor Gary Horton, potter Mike De Haan, glass artist Vicki Fanning, photographer Di Halsted and printer Sandy Meharry, belong to the group.

The Mahurangi Group has a core of well-established artists from the region who get together to show their work in an exhibition every two years. Members include Terry Stringer, Barry Lett (artwork pictured opposite) and Mike Petre. They usually invite other well-respected artists to exhibit with them, and the venue for their shows change from exhibition to exhibition. These shows are highly rated by the art world.

MORRIS & JAMES POTTERY

OMAHA GALLERY

Anthony Morris and his family returned to New Zealand from Britain in 1977 to establish their family business at Matakana. For several years they produced terracotta pots using the supply of iron-rich clay on their property, which previously had been used for brick-making. But by the mid-1980s the pottery was producing pots and tiles with brightly coloured glazes, putting Matakana on the map as visitors came from afar to source their distinctive works.

Today, their wonderfully large gallery and showroom is filled with pots, wall art and sculptural pieces. Each work is individually hand-decorated using rich, vibrant colours.

Tongue Farm Rd, Matakana, ph: (09) 422 7116, www.morrisandjames.co.nz

Mark Brockie and Chrissy Purdom's gallery is situated near the Omaha estuary, close to the causeway. They have developed the gallery to extend beyond their own works, and feature art, sculpture and ceramics from local artists, and some from further afield.

They also stock carefully selected furniture, wall art and lighting and a range of gifts.

327 Omaha Flats Rd, Omaha Beach, ph: (09) 422 9294, www.omahagallery.co.nz

PIECE GALLERY

ZEALANDIA SCULPTURE GARDEN

This contemporary gallery occupies a beautiful, light-filled space on the river's edge in the Matakana Village complex. Owner Emma Haughton, who has a fine arts degree and worked in film for 15 years, has impeccable taste in selecting objects of art to display and sell in her gallery. She sources pieces from around New Zealand and locally, including a diverse selection of ceramics and domestic pieces, woven work, contemporary jewellery, cast and blown glass, wooden pieces and designer floor rugs.

Exhibitions are held throughout the year, both solo or group shows, with interesting and quirky themes.

2 Matakana Valley Rd, Matakana Village,
ph: (09) 422 9125

A private sculpture garden in Mahurangi West established by well-known sculptor Terry Stringer, the garden has been conceived to surprise visitors with a sculptural vision of the surrounding pastoral landscape. Stringer's own works are displayed, along with selected pieces by other artists.

Open on weekends from November to March and by appointment, the garden has a small admission charge, with guided tours that include a coffee break.

138 Mahurangi West Rd, Warkworth,
ph: (09) 422 0099,
www.zealandiasculpturegarden.co.nz

OUTDOOR
ADVENTURER

Some of the best-kept secrets of the region are the unspoilt beaches and coastal walks. I find it hard to leave Omaha Beach, as often I can have the beach almost to myself mid-week or on a stormy day, but there are so many lovely places to explore that it's always rewarding to get out and about. Getting into the car is the hardest part.

REGIONAL PARKS

Three parks administered and supervised by the Auckland Regional Council can be found within 20 minutes of Matakana Village.

Mahurangi Regional Park
This park is split into three distinct areas, each accessed separately. Mahurangi West is the largest area and is approached by taking the Mahurangi West Rd (off State Highway 1), then turning on to Ngarewa Drive. There are three pohutukawa-fringed bays for swimming, but only the largest of these, Sullivan's or Otarawao, is accessible by car. The other two, Mita Bay and Te Muri Bay, are worth the walk, as the tracks pass through native bush and, in the case of Te Muri, across an estuary at low tide. Camping at all three beaches is by permit only.

The second part of this park is Scott Point, accessed along Ridge Rd, near Scotts Landing. The historic Scott Homestead is a favourite stop for boaties year round as there is plenty of water for anchoring off the point.

The third area of the park, Mahurangi East, is accessible only by sea, so those with boats can enjoy the tranquility and remote location.

OPPOSITE: **Mahurangi Regional Park**

163

OPPOSITE: Scandrett Bay

Scandrett Regional Park

On the southern edge of Kawau Bay and reached by the road that passes along the Mahurangi Peninsula through Snells Beach, Scandrett Regional Park is named for the family who farmed the land for more than 130 years. This is an ideal destination for a picnic. The park has coastal forest, rocky headlands, a sandy beach, farmland and historic farm buildings, which are being restored. The park also boasts some spectacular old pohutukawa trees.

A well-marked walk leads out to Mullet Point along the cliffs, providing wide views of the bay and over to Kawau Island. Walkers can take a different route back to the car park. Mountain biking is allowed, but there are no campsites.

OPPOSITE: Anchor Bay

Tawharanui Regional Park

This lovely park can be found at the end of the Takatu Peninsula. The last six kilometres of the road is narrow, unsealed and winding, but the trip is worth every minute spent in the car. It's a favourite picnic spot as the 588-hectare park has some pristine, white-sand, north-facing beaches, including the popular Anchor Bay. There are also plenty of shady spots close to the beach for relaxation and passing a day away.

The park has basic-level campsites, but campers must obtain a pass before they pitch their tents. Campervans and caravans can stay overnight for a maximum of two nights in selected car parks.

For walkers, there are several well-marked and maintained tracks that pass through bush or follow the coastline and the cliffs on the south side of the peninsula. Brochures are available identifying the flora and fauna. Most walks take between one and a half and three hours.

A special feature of Tawharanui is the fact it is an open sanctuary, protected by a 2.5km predator-proof fence. A locally formed group of supporters, Tawharanui Open Sanctuary Society Incorporated (TOSSI), raises funds and assists with pest eradication, public education and restoration of wetlands and forest. This group also coordinates an annual art exhibition as a fund-raiser (see page 146).

On the northern coast of the park, the open sanctuary is bordered by a marine park that is marvellous for snorkelling, but no fish or marine life can be taken from this area.

RESERVES

OPPOSITE: Goat Island in the Leigh Marine Reserve

Kawau Island Historic Reserve

A short ferry or water-taxi ride from the Sandspit Wharf will take you to Kawau Island's Bon Accord Harbour. The historic reserve takes up about one-tenth of the island and is managed by the Department of Conservation. This is the site of Mansion House, the grand home bought by Governor Sir George Grey in 1862. He enlarged the house and established Italianate gardens there — the conifers and other exotic trees, peacocks and wallabies in the grounds are his legacy.

The house, which can be visited for a small entrance fee, has been extensively restored by DOC and furnished in the style of Grey's era.

The park and walks are open to visitors, but no camping or accommodation is available in the park. However, there are some private holiday homes for rent on the island.

Well-signposted walks to other historic places on the island include tracks to Coppermine Bay, Momona Point and Schoolhouse Bay.

Leigh Marine Reserve

This reserve, often known as Goat Island after the small island just off the beach that is part of the reserve, has been a popular picnic spot for many years. The University of Auckland's science department has a marine research laboratory here.

The area is perfect for diving and snorkelling, and equipment can be hired close by. Glass-bottomed boat trips are available for those who don't wish to get wet while observing the teeming sea life.

There are two walking tracks at the reserve: the Cape Rodney Track, which is about a two-hour round trip to the cape past the research station, and the Pakiri Track, which leads to the superb Pakiri Beach, but is sometimes not accessible at high tide.

OTHER WALKING TRACKS

OPPOSITE: The Ti Point
Walkway

There is a wealth of walking tracks throughout the Matakana area and the surrounding region. At the information centres in Warkworth and at the Matakana Cinemas, visitors can pick up a copy of *Walking Tracks in Rodney District*, a very well-researched brochure issued by the Rodney District Council.

Almost every beach has a walkway and, although the tracks in the regional parks are hard to beat, my favourites are the walk around the seabird sanctuary at the mouth of the Whangateau Harbour at Omaha, the two-hour coastal walkway around the foreshore at Ti Point, and especially the Mt Tamahunga walkway on Omaha Valley Rd for its magnificent views up and down the coast.

For the tramper who really likes a challenge, the track from the Dome Forest car park to Govan Wilson Rd is a seven-hour hike. It is part of Te Araroa — 'the long pathway' — which, by the time it is completed in 2010, will provide a track to walk the length of New Zealand.

Other Te Araroa walks in the region include the Tamahunga tramp, the Dunn's Bush and Ridge tramp near Puhoi, and the Okura Bush walkway on the coast from the Weiti River, south of the Whangaparoa Peninsula, to the Okura River.

For many years the region surrounding Matakana has been known as a northern holiday playground, as the beaches and balmy climate attract sun-seekers and the many harbours and calm waters in the region are perfect for watersports. It's certainly what has drawn me to the area, and I revel in being able to swim from Labour Day through to Queen's Birthday weekend (no wetsuit, either!). As well as those already mentioned in this chapter, beaches not to miss include the following:

BEACHES

OPPOSITE: Martins Bay

Mahurangi East Peninsula Beaches

There are some lovely swimming beaches on the north side of this peninsula overlooking Kawau Bay.

- Brick Bay, a tiny, unpopulated reserve with shady trees and a sandy beach with a shallow seabed, can be accessed from Kauri Drive at Sandspit.

- Snells Beach is well populated, with a wide expanse of sand, especially at low tide when the water recedes into the distance.

- Algies Bay is another popular built-up beach with a sandy coastline and many permanent residents and holiday-makers.

- Martins Bay, towards the end of the peninsula before Scandrett Regional Park, is a safe, sandy swimming beach with some lovely pohutukawa for shade.

Scotts Landing is on the southern side of the peninsula and has a small beach, but is better known by boaties than swimmers.

Matheson Bay

A small but popular beach with a small community of weekenders and holiday-makers who stay in baches with great views to Little Barrier Island and the outer Hauraki Gulf.

Omaha Beach

In the centre of this magnificent beach the surf club patrols an area for public swimming. There are changing facilities and toilets at the beach, which is well populated with permanent residents and holiday homes. The bird sanctuary at the northern end provides a haven for dotterels, fairy terns and oystercatchers to breed.

OPPOSITE: Pakiri Beach

Pakiri Beach

Although the route to Pakiri requires driving on unsealed road for part of the journey, the magnificent sweep of pristine sand makes this the most outstanding beach in the region. It's a surf beach, although there is a small estuary at the south end that's ideal for families with smaller children who like to swim. Horse riding here is fantastic, as there's nothing quite like riding along a seemingly endless white sandy beach. There's also a good camping ground at the southern end of the beach.

Takatu Peninsula beaches

On the south-facing coast of the Takatu Peninsula there is a series of small beaches with holiday houses facing Kawau Bay. Fishing, sailing and swimming are the popular pastimes here. Look for Buckleton, Campbells and Baddeleys Beaches, although the privately owned beaches further along the peninsula have no public access.

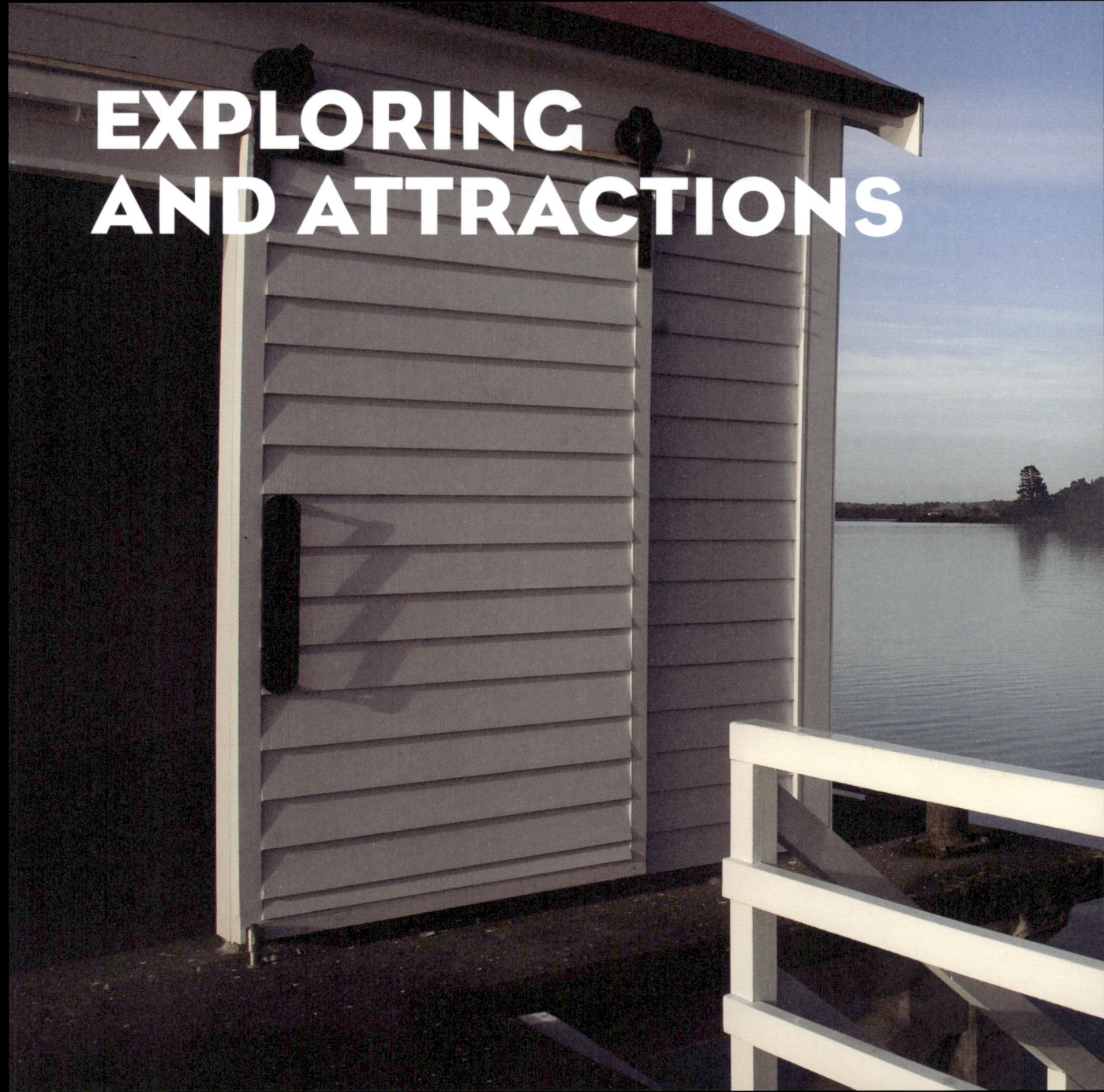

EXPLORING AND ATTRACTIONS

When I think about the attractions of Matakana, I dream of the food and wine, closely followed by the beaches, parks and walks. And the farmers' market is so well known as a destination it is hard to remember it began only in 2004.

But there are plenty of other activities to check out, and the local information centres at Warkworth and Matakana have details of these. Some of the special attractions are listed here, along with tours and transport options. It is a rural area, however, so there is no regular public transport, but there are two taxi companies which can be booked for trips around the district.

EXPLORING AND ATTRACTIONS

Matakana Village

Architect Noel Lane has bestowed on the township a stunningly understated complex, with finishes and details that most developers would shun in favour of economy, thus setting a new standard for a rural centre. The high-quality retail shops, a cinema complex, restaurant, wine bar and a variety of other spaces leased to local businesses are surrounded by beautifully planted gardens and paving. The farmers' market, held every Saturday morning throughout the year, is tucked into the corner of this site.

The Matakana Cinemas are drop-dead gorgeous, with top technology and dazzling design in the three different theatres. Premium-release movies run on a full timetable with something for everyone throughout the day.

The standard of the retail and speciality stores in the Village is exceptional, with women's and men's fashion and shoe stores, a florist, beauty stores, gift stores, an art gallery, a home décor store, a chocolaterie and a pharmacy. My personal favourites are The Village Bookshop, with its wonderful range of books and cosy interior; Red Letter Day, a store dedicated to penmanship; and Stubbs Village Butchery, which is packed with all the deli and store-cupboard items I need. The restaurant, fish and chip store, wine bar, and ice-cream and coffee café all provide delights to tempt the appetite.

On the adjoining section of the main street are a general store, a café, a hardware store and Bach, a surf and beach accessory store. Further up Matakana Valley Rd, the excellent Matakana Patisserie sits among some light-industrial buildings.

Matakana Country Park

The Matakana Country Park is the brainchild of an enterprising local, John Baker, who wished to re-create some of his own childhood rural experiences for the next generation to enjoy. The property borders both the Leigh and Omaha Flats roads and offers a wide variety of activities and adventures.

The buildings, reminiscent of a large farm station, house an art gallery, the excellent Country Kitchen Café, a craft shop, the RD6 restaurant and a superb gymnasium, The Circuit Room.

The grounds cover about 20 hectares, all with recent plantings. For outdoor-minded visitors there is an equestrian centre, horse and pony riding for children, a children's adventure playground, a miniature railway and animals including a kunekune pig, llamas, goats and donkeys that children can feed.

On Saturday mornings there's a country market in the main building and the outside courtyard where local craftsmen and growers ply their wares. At the height of the summer holidays, an outdoor cinema shows current movies.

The most recent addition is the tiny, historic St Andrew's Presbyterian Church, built in 1895, which has been restored and is available for weddings, christenings, funerals and small events.

EXPLORING AND ATTRACTIONS

OPPOSITE: Parry Kauri Park

The Honey Centre

This café and store devoted to honey is on State Highway 1, about five kilometres south of Warkworth. A great place to stop for a break and keep the children amused.

Pakiri Beach Horse Rides

Bookings are essential for the variety of horse-riding options at Pakiri Beach. Rides range from one-hour through to seven-day, coast-to-coast adventures on horseback. Accommodation is also offered.

Parry Kauri Park

This magnificent stand of bush off Thompson Rd, just south of Warkworth, has a loop walking track, the Kauri Bushmen's Walkway, that leads visitors past two magnificient kauri trees, one close to 1000 years old. And there are dozens more kauri and other native trees to be admired along the short pathway. Also visit the Warkworth and District Museum situated in the park.

Puriri Tree Country Estate

An eco-store, with New Zealand gifts and souvenirs, is the centre of this adventure park about four kilometres north of Matakana on the Leigh road. Archery, paintball, corporate team-building activities and children's bush-survival training are offered.

SheepWorld

Working dogs show off their skills at this sheep farm and nature park with a café and shop, four kilometres north of Warkworth on State Highway 1. Activities include an eco-discovery trail and feeding farm animals.

Villa Tamahunga

A beautiful display garden and olive grove in Omaha Valley Rd, open on the first Sunday of each month from October to April or by appointment.

EXPLORING AND ATTRACTIONS

OPPOSITE: Wilson
Cement Works ruins

Wilson Cement Works

The historic cement works in Wilson Rd, Warkworth, are named after their founder, Nathaniel Wilson. The works operated from 1872 until 1928 and the ruins are worth visiting as a reminder of the pioneering history of the area. A good picnic spot with a freshwater swimming hole that's popular in the summer.

Golf courses

Two golf courses in the Matakana area are open to the public and non-members are welcome. Omaha Beach Golf Club, which borders the Omaha estuary, has nine original holes (that are constantly being upgraded) to the left of the causeway and nine further holes developed more recently with the subdivision of the south end of Omaha, creating a full, interesting and challenging course. It is a delight to play, as several holes on the second part of the course have walkways through the bush reserves, and the last four holes play up the edge of the estuary.

Warkworth Golf Club is on the main road between Warkworth and Matakana and is a pleasant rural course with some challenging hills that afford good views.

Food and wine tours

Wine lovers can visit wineries, imbibe and leave the driving to a professional.
Wisdome Tours, ph: (09) 423 9558
Warkworth Tours, ph: (09) 422 2505
Warkworth Taxi and Minibus Charter, ph: (09) 425 0000

Matakabs

Local taxi and transport for regional tours, winery tours and local and airport service in environmentally friendly hybrid vehicles.
Ph: (09) 422 2244

Skytours Helicopters

A locally based helicopter service for sightseeing and charter flights.
Ph: (09) 422 7018

189

WHERE TO STAY

With so much to see around Matakana, visitors can happily spend several days exploring, walking, shopping, visiting wineries, discovering beaches and experiencing other recreational pursuits. In the past few years a crop of accommodation options, from small B&Bs to luxury lodges, have sprung up in every part of the region. Two places cater for larger groups, whether for a conference or if a celebration is called for: Kourawhero Country Lodge, with 18 suites, and the Quest Matakana, which has 17 villas.

It's always wise to make reservations ahead to ensure a good night's sleep. The i-Site information centre in Warkworth is always helpful, with accommodation listings to suit every budget.

Alegria Beautyfarm

Claudia Schenz offers a range of beauty treatments and accommodation for up to four people in two rooms in her purpose-built retreat, situated high on a ridge overlooking vines with wide views of the countryside. Trained in beauty therapy in Germany, Claudia is also an excellent cook and bakes German-style bread, pastries and savoury items for an excellent breakfast as part of the package. Large swimming pool on site.

**180 Monarch Downs Way,
ph: (09) 422 7211, www.beautyfarm.co.nz**

Castle Matakana

Luxury B&B accommodation with three large suites, all with magnificent views over the surrounding countryside. A tiny vineyard on the property produces the house wine and gourmet breakfast is served each morning.

**378 Whitmore Rd, Matakana,
ph: (09) 422 9288,
www.the-castle.co.nz**

WHERE TO STAY

Gifford Lodge

This architecturally designed lodge with accommodation for up to 10 people is situated on a hilltop in a rural setting with wide views. The lodge is about three kilometres from Warkworth, just off the Matakana Rd. Weddings, functions and small conferences are catered for. Fine breakfasts are served, and dinner is by arrangement.

**139 Clayden Rd, Warkworth,
ph: (09) 425 9995,
www.giffordlodge.co.nz**

Hurstmere House

A gracious 1920s-style house in a rural setting only two minutes from the centre of Matakana village. Four suites are available at this B&B, operated by the owners of Tapiano Bar & Bistro in the village.

**186 Tongue Farm Rd, Matakana,
ph: (09) 422 9220**

Kourawhero Country Lodge

With 18 deluxe suites, a spa, gymnasium, pool, bush walks, a well-qualified gourmet chef and conference and function facilities,

Kourawhero Country Lodge is ideal for groups looking for a retreat. It is situated at the top of a valley to the southwest of Warkworth, overlooking farmland with views to Kawau and Little Barrier islands and the Hauraki Gulf. The suites are set in clusters around the estate and each is well appointed. Kourawhero also has its own 17.7 metre charter boat for day cruising and fishing.

**471 Wyllie Rd, Kourawhero, Warkworth,
ph: (09) 422 3377, www.kourawhero.co.nz**

Leigh Sawmill

The Leigh Sawmill Café is a restaurant and bar that has become almost legendary over the years among locals and visitors as a place to eat, drink and enjoy great musical gigs. Adjacent to the main building there are five private suites that are basic, but comfortably furnished and private. There is also backpacker accommodation in bunk rooms with self-catering facilities.

**142 Pakiri Road, Leigh, ph: (09) 422 6019,
www.sawmillcafe.co.nz**

Quest Matakana

Seventeen fully self-contained and serviced villas are set among vines and olive trees on a 15-hectare riverside estate about five minutes from the Matakana Village. Features include a swimming pool, tennis court, private boat-ramp and jetty and outdoor decks on all villas. No catering on site, but breakfast packs can be delivered.

170 Green Rd, Matakana, ph: (09) 423 0353, www.questmatakana.co.nz

Rosemount Homestead

An elegant 100-year-old kauri villa set in well-tended gardens, with rural and vineyard views. Three en suite rooms, a swimming pool, library and a delicious country-style breakfast make this an excellent B&B with a friendly host who knows the area well.

25 Rosemount Rd, Warkworth, ph: (09) 422 2580, www.rosemount.co.nz

Sugarloaf Lodge

A stylish B&B high above the Omaha Flats on rural land overlooking Little Barrier Island and the Hauraki Gulf, with two generous double bedroom suites, separated from the main house. Fully cooked breakfasts and a complimentary glass of local wine in the evening.

1068 Leigh Rd, Matakana, ph: (09) 422 9515, www.sugarloaflodge.co.nz

Takatu Lodge

This lodge has a spectacular setting in the midst of the Takatu vineyard, with four luxury suites, two with private decks, adjacent to the vines. It is centrally located, just off the Tawharanui Rd and close to Matakana village and the Country Park. Superb breakfasts, pre-dinner wine tasting and nibbles in the evening, and dinner at the lodge can be cooked by a private chef by arrangement.

518 Whitmore Rd, Matakana, ph: (09) 423 0299, www.takatulodge.co.nz

Tera del Mar

A grand Victorian-style house set on the Leigh ridge, with spectacular views over Pakiri Beach. Outdoor spa, guest lounge, five comfortable bedrooms and landscaped gardens.

140 Rodney Rd, Leigh, ph: (09) 422 6090, www.teradelmar.co.nz

WHERE TO STAY

OPPOSITE, CLOCKWISE FROM TOP LEFT: Quest Matakana; Ti Point Retreat; The Saltings Guest House; Rosemount Homestead

The Beach House Resort

This private retreat at Vivian Bay, Kawau Island's largest sandy beach, is a haven away from the mainland. Accessible by water taxi, the lodge has 10 fully equipped suites, which face onto either the beach or a courtyard. Breakfast and a three-course dinner are included in the tariff.

Vivian Bay, Kawau Island, ph: (09) 422 8850, www.kawauresort.co.nz

The Saltings Guest House

Boutique B&B accommodation is offered in three suites in the original lodge, perched high above the Sandspit road, overlooking the estuary and harbour. Close by, on the estate vineyard, self-contained, self-catering apartments are available in the Vintner's Haven.

1210 Sandspit Rd, Matakana, ph: (09) 425 9670, www.saltings.co.nz

Ti Point Retreat

A stylish home in a private location, overlooking the sweep of Omaha Beach, with huge decks and expanses of glass to take in the stunning views. Can be booked as a private hideaway for four, or as a B&B arrangement, as the owner lives in an adjacent apartment.

Ti Point Rd, Ti Point, Leigh, ph: (09) 422 6908, www.tipointretreat.co.nz

Waimana Point Lodge

Set on a headland above Martins Bay at the end of the Mahurangi East peninsula, this is a secluded lodge offering luxury accommodation. A stylish building with four well-appointed, self-contained suites with private patios and a walkway to the beach. Breakfasts are delivered to each suite and dinner, featuring local produce, can be served on request.

35 Martins Bay Road, Warkworth, ph: (09) 425 5102, www.waimanapoint.co.nz

Waipiata Boutique Lodge

Nestled in native trees on the western shores of the Mahurangi, this Noel Lane-designed luxury property offers two beautifully appointed suites. The lodge is set on 160 hectares of rolling farmland and native kauri forest with several kilometres of coastline. Excellent breakfasts, wine and dinner can be arranged.

657 Pukapuka Rd, Mahurangi West, ph: (09) 422 0156, www.waipiata.co.nz

EATING AND SNACKING

200

There are plenty of eating-out options in the Matakana area, from simple takeout picnic fare from the cafés and patisserie to the casual food at the legendary Leigh Sawmill Café and smart tapas in relaxed surroundings at the Matakana Village. Visitors should remember that this is a rural area, with no ready pool of professional wait-staff to call on. Service is likely to be friendly and helpful, but without the polish that might be expected in an urban area.

Likewise, there's only a small permanent population and, while business is brisk over the holiday periods, the rest of the year can provide lean pickings for the hospitality trade. There's a ready turnover in this type of business, so it will pay to check out the opening hours before setting out for any chosen eating destination.

Just relax and enjoy the country!

Ascension Vineyard

An imposing Tuscan-styled winery complex with a large dining area overlooking a formal garden and petanque court. The atmosphere is casual, but the food is serious, with grilled meats, poultry and a full menu designed to match the wines. An adjoining dedicated reception and conference centre makes this a popular venue for weddings and corporate groups, and from time to time there are musical gigs on site.
480 Matakana Road, Matakana, ph: (09) 422 9601

Black Dog Coffee and Country Kitchen

With its outdoor seating area this is the ideal place to have breakfast and read the paper. Popular with locals and open throughout the day in Matakana Valley Rd, next to the general store.
23 Matakana Valley Road, Matakana, ph: (09) 422 9130

OPPOSITE: Black Dog, Matakana

EATING AND SNACKING

Blue

A busy café right on the Matakana roundabout and in front of the cinemas, serving organic ice-creams, sorbets and frozen fresh fruit yoghurt, coffee, toasted sandwiches, cake and more. It is busy throughout the year. Don't miss the frozen blueberry yoghurt made with organic blueberries from the Omaha Blueberries farm.

2 Matakana Valley Road, Matakana, ph: (09) 422 7797

Brookview Teahouse

The delicious home-style, locally sourced food makes this my number one choice of eating establishment in the region. Across the road from the Matakana Cinemas, at the roundabout, the teahouse is in a superbly decorated 1920s bungalow. It has a charming collection of old china and a relaxed, happy atmosphere. The star of the menu is the tiered Brookview Tea, with little sandwiches, savouries, delicate cakes and tea, coffee or champagne.

1335 Leigh Road, Matakana, ph: (09) 423 0390

Café Sandspit

This truly is a seaside café, perched at the end of the Sandspit Wharf, with lovely views. Open for brunch and lunch and serving dinner on days that vary seasonally. Famous for fresh fish and chips and creamy seafood chowder.

Sandspit Wharf, 1440 Sandspit Road, Warkworth, ph: (09) 425 9475

Charlies Gelato Garden

This relaxing little café serves freshly made gelato and sorbets on a flower-decorated veranda about 250 metres up Sharp Rd from Matakana Rd. It is part of a strawberry and grape garden so customers can purchase freshly picked fruit in season. A Fine Line Gallery on the same site holds regular exhibitions.

17 Sharp Rd, Matakana, ph: (09) 422 7942

Cosí at Morris & James

The tiles and colourful pots from the adjoining pottery have been put to good use in this charming casual café. Dean Betts, who runs this café with his wife Toni, makes great use of seasonal organic produce, which takes pride of place on the menu along with local fish and wine from the vineyards in the Matakana area. A very relaxing place to meet friends for coffee or a more substantial meal. Dinners on Friday nights only.

Tongue Farm Rd, Matakana, ph: (09) 422 7116

EATING AND SNACKING

OPPOSITE TOP: Leigh Sawmill Café

OPPOSITE BELOW: Heron's Flight

Country Kitchen Café

A cheerful little café in the main building of the Matakana Country Park. Good coffee and nice home-baked goodies and sandwiches served throughout the day.
Matakana Country Park, Omaha Flats Rd, Matakana, ph: (09) 422 7133

The Diner

Delicious hamburgers and fish and chips are made to order in this casual café on the Omaha Beach causeway. Formerly the Pohutukawa Café.
Omaha Flats Rd, Omaha, ph: (09) 423 0365

Heron's Flight

A newly constructed villa is the setting for this winery restaurant on Sharp Rd. The dining area looks over tranquil countryside and the gardens reflect the history of the area. A modern menu of delicious food is designed to enhance the wines. Open for lunch, with dinner served on selected evenings.
49 Sharp Rd, Matakana, ph: (09) 422 7915

Leigh Fish and Chips

A casual little fish and chip outlet in Leigh that is popular with locals and passers-by returning from the Leigh Marine Reserve.

18 Cumberland Street, Leigh, ph: (09) 422 6035

Leigh Sawmill Café

Famous for woodfired pizza, fresh fish from the nearby Leigh Fisheries and frequent musical gigs that sometimes use the concert grand piano, this is a wonderfully casual restaurant on the Pakiri Rd at Leigh. It has become a dining destination to spend an afternoon in the gardens, view the memorabilia collection and try the beers from the micro-brewery on site. Local organic produce features on the menu and children are well catered for. Accommodation available.
142 Pakiri Rd, Leigh, ph: (09) 422 6019

Mariposa Palm Gardens Café and Nursery

Tables are set al fresco among the palms in a large shade house. The property, which also serves as a palm nursery, can be found down a long palm-lined driveway on the main road into Point Wells from Omaha Flats. Sandwiches, quiche and country-style fare are made on the premises daily. A haven in all weathers.
253 Point Wells Rd, Point Wells, Matakana, ph: (09) 422 7597

EATING AND SNACKING

Matakana Country House

This historic pub that has served Matakana for more than a century has great pub-style food in very casual surroundings, with plenty of outdoor tables. Check out the historic photos within.
Matakana Valley Rd, Matakana, ph: (09) 422 9770

Matakana Fish and Chips

A fairly upmarket fish and chip shop in the Matakana Village complex, fronting on to the main street.
2 Matakana Valley Rd, Matakana, ph: (09) 422 7889

Matakana Patisserie

There are tables and bench seating at this popular bakery and café about 400 metres up Matakana Valley Rd. Good sourdough breads, terrific pies and lovely pastries to accompany coffee.
70 Matakana Valley Rd, Matakana, ph: (09) 422 9896

RD6

This rustic country restaurant is housed in a large space with a country barn feel in the Matakana Country Park. It continues to serve lunches and dinners featuring hearty food.
1 Omaha Flats Rd, Matakana, ph: (09) 422 7360

Rusty Pelican Restaurant, Bar and Pizzeria

A longtime favourite haunt of locals, serving meals and particularly good pizzas every day and evening. Fully licensed and run in conjunction with the Rusty Tui Sports Bar next door. Rustic surroundings on the roundabout at Matakana.
1001 Matakana Rd, Matakana, ph: (09) 422 9122

Tapiano Bar & Bistro

This tapas bar and bistro (formerly the Matakana Brasserie), downstairs in the Matakana Village complex, offers relaxed lunches and dinners, with a separate area for tapas designed with cinema-goers in mind. There's an extensive wine list and lovely outdoor dining by the river in warm weather. A piano for entertainment as well.
2 Matakana Valley Rd, Matakana, ph: (09) 423 0383

The Vintry

A comfortable wine bar in the Matakana Cinemas complex serving locally produced wines. Plates of tapas can be ordered to accompany the wines and tasting flights are available.
2 Matakana Valley Road, Matakana, ph: (09) 423 0251

SURROUNDING MATAKANA

Puhoi

Puhoi, a small village town with a long history, was settled in the mid-nineteenth century by a group of Bohemians who left Prague to make their new home in isolation on the far side of the world. Their only contact with the outside world came when the regular coastal trading boats called in to the wharf on the Puhoi riverbank. These early settlers earned their livelihood felling extensive stands of giant kauri trees to provide building materials for growing Auckland city, just as their neighbours in Matakana did in earlier times.

Today, this is an interesting hamlet to visit. It is south of Warkworth and worth the short detour — about a kilometre's drive — from the main highway north. The most-visited establishment is probably the Puhoi Hotel, a real country pub that was built in 1879 and is still the heart of the community. An excellent museum (formerly the convent school), a quaint library and several other significant buildings can also be found in the township. Other traditional colonial wooden buildings, such as the Catholic church dating back to 1881, are still in use.

Visitors may be lucky enough to catch a performance of Bohemian dancing at events and festivities in the town, for the descendants of the original settlers have kept this tradition going.

There are several small cafés, hearty meals at the pub and a couple of speciality stores, one selling mustard and another selling cheese. Puhoi is also a centre for river trips by kayak, and the keen and fit may like to paddle all the way to the rivermouth at the Wenderholm Regional Park.

OPPOSITE: Puhoi hotel interior

THIS PAGE: The historic Puhoi Catholic church

211

Warkworth

This picturesque town, just south of Matakana on State Highway 1, is the busy hub and business centre of Rodney district. With plenty of history, the town has some lovely old buildings throughout its centre. The Heritage Trail, an easy walk of about 90 minutes, passes by most of these original or restored buildings and can be followed with a brochure from the information centre.

The main access to the town in the early years of coastal transport was via the Mahurangi River, which opens on to the upper reaches of the Mahurangi Harbour. The river meanders along behind the main shopping street and an attractive walkway has been built for visitors who come to feed the town's much-loved ducks and relax on the tranquil riverbank.

The retail shops in the town are many and varied, and include a large supermarket and many speciality stores. Scattered throughout the centre are many cafés and restaurants, and several accommodation options are to be found nearby. The Warkworth i-Site Visitor Information Centre, in the town centre at 1 Baxter St, is a first stop when visiting the region, as volunteers and permanent staff are very friendly and helpful.

The town supports the surrounding district with a full-range of businesses and service industries.

Snells Beach and Mahurangi East

The residential area at Snells Beach is supported by the Mahurangi shopping centre, a small retail and light-industrial centre that services the Mahurangi East peninsula, offering fishing and diving supplies, a service station, restaurants and takeaways, and a large all-purpose store serving nearby communities at Algies Bay, Whisper Cove, Sandspit, Scotts Landing and Martins Bay.

Plenty of accommodation can be found in the area, including The Salty Dog Inn, with a charming old English atmosphere and 14 rooms. The Scandrett Regional Park and the eastern part of the Mahurangi Regional Park are accessed by the main road that passes along the peninsula.

Sandspit is the departure point for ferries and water taxis to Kawau Island, which dominates the Kawau Bay area. There's a pleasant café on the Sandspit Wharf.

OPPOSITE: Masonic Hall, Warkworth

213

SURROUNDING MATAKANA

OPPOSITE: Leigh
harbour

Whangateau, Omaha Beach and Point Wells

The drive along the coastal road from Matakana to Leigh passes the inlets of
the Whangateau Harbour. It's a pretty drive, past many coastal properties with
lovely views over the water to the communities at Omaha and Point Wells. Take
a detour about a kilometre north from the Matakana village to visit Omaha
Beach and the small residential and retirement community at Point Wells.

Omaha Beach has seen a huge growth in homes for weekenders, holiday-
makers and permanent residents over the past six years since the south end
of the beach was subdivided. The original subdivision at the north end also
continues to grow, as it has for more than 30 years. The community centre,
which serves the golf club and the bowling club, has a café serving snacks and
lunches through the day and dinner on weekends. Not to be missed are the
five large carved Maori pou whenua that guard the southern community. The
most important, Omaha, stands on the corner of Mangatawhiri Drive, and the
others line the beach in the sand dunes.

Point Wells has lovely properties that border the estuary. It is a community
of mainly permanent residents, with a few weekenders. A store, tennis courts
and a community hall are used by locals. At Whangateau there's a camping
ground and a sports field, but no store.

Leigh, Ti Point and Matheson Bay

The northern sector of the Matakana region is marked by the tiny community
of Leigh, with both holiday homes and permanent residential properties. The
town, the gateway to the Leigh Marine Reserve, is well known for its fish and
chips and the Leigh Sawmill Café. Also central to the town is the Leigh Fisheries processing plant, from where some of New Zealand's finest and freshest
fish is sent away to restaurants around the country and overseas each day.

Ti Point Rd, just before Matheson Bay, leads to the Ti Point Wharf and the
Ti Point Scenic Reserve, which is accessed by a coastal track. A reptile park,
about 400 metres along the road, has a collection of live lizards, iguanas,
turtles, chameleons and tuatara. It's a great place to take children who are
interested in rarely seen reptiles.

Matheson Bay is a community of mainly weekenders and holiday homes. On
the foreshore is a pleasant reserve with children's play equipment, and the
beach is safe for swimming in most weather conditions.

ACCOMMODATION AND ATTRACTIONS

1 Alegria Beauty farm
2 Castle Matakana
3 Gifford Lodge
4 Hurstmere House
5 Kourawhero Country Lodge
6 Leigh Sawmill
7 Quest Matakana
8 Rosemount Homestead
9 Sugar Loaf B&B
10 Takatu Lodge
11 Tera del Mar
12 The Beach House Resort
13 The Saltings
14 Ti Point Retreat
15 Waimana Point Lodge
16 Waipiata Boutique Lodge
17 Matakana Country Park
18 Matakana Village
19 Omaha Golf Course
20 Pakiri Beach Horse Riding
21 Parry Kauri Park
22 Puriri Country Estate
23 Sheepworld
24 The Honey Centre
25 Villa Tamahunga
26 Warkworth Golf Course
27 Wilson's Cement Works

WELLSFORD

PAKIRI

Goat Island

LEIGH

WHANGATEAU

Matheson Bay

TI POINT

POINT WELLS

OMAHA

Omaha Bay

MATAKANA

Whangateau Harbour

Tokatu Point

Tawharanui Peninsula

North Channel

Baddeleys Beach

SANDSPIT

BON Accord Harbour

KAWAU ISLAND

SNELLS BEACH

Bucketons Beach

Brick Bay

Kawau Bay

Algies Bay

Scandrett Bay

Mansion House

Mahurangi River

ARKWORTH

Martins Bay

Beehive Island (Taungamaro Is.)

Motuketekete Is.

Moturekareka Is.

Scotts Landing

Te Haupa Is.

Motuora Is.

MAHURANGI WEST

Mahurangi Harbour

UHOI

GROWERS AND PRODUCERS

BUSINESS NAME	CONTACT	PHONE	ADDRESS	AREA
Andrews Organics	Andrew Rochford	09 425 7629	162 Goatley Rd	Warkworth
Ascension Vineyard Ltd	Darryl Soljan	09 422 9601	480 Matakana Road	Matakana
Big Cock Vineyard (Oleanz Estates Ltd)	Rachel Dawson	09 422 7206	Matakana Road	Matakana
Biomarine Ltd	Jim Dollimore	09 425 5076	Snells Beach	Warkworth
Blue Icecream Café (Omaha Bluberries)	Robert & Shannon Auton	09 422 7797	Matakana Valley Rd	Matakana
Brick Bay Wines	Christine & Richard Didsbury	09 425 4690	Arabella Lane	Snells Beach
Contour Estate	Bruce & Linsey-Ann Taylor	09 423 0002	139 Takatu Road	Matakana
De Vine Chocolat	Jill Kessner	09 422 9232	2 Matakana Valley Road	Matakana
Echo Valley Olives	Don Windley & Teresa Anderson	09 488 0902	59 Echo Valley Rd RD	Mangawhai
Elocin Speciality Foods	Nicole Tucker	09 425 9593	Glenmore Drive	Warkworth
Fresh Food Exports Ltd	John Greensworth	09 422 7006	256 Omaha Flats Rd	Omaha
Greve Vineyard	Peter & Lorraine Carpenter	09 422 7744	191 Takatu Road RD6	Matakana
Hawks Nest Vineyard	Lynette Smith		646 Matakana Road	Matakana
Heron's Flight Vineyard & Café	Mary Evans	09 422 7915	49 Sharp Road	Matakana
Hill Foot Farm	Peter & Katie Mitchell	09 422 5042	603 Old Woodcocks Road	Warkworth
Hillbeck Gardens/Charlies Gelato Garden & Vineyard	Charlie Wigglesworth	09 422 7980	Sharp Road	Matakana
Hincho Winery	Andrea & Mike Hinchco	09 422 7200	150 Monarch Downs Way	Warkworth
Homefresh	Caroline Beamish	09 422 7234	Sharp Road	Matakana
Honey Centre & Honey Café Ltd	Rod Clarke	09 425 8003	7 Perry Rd	Warkworth
Hyperion Wines	John & Jill Crone	09 422 9375	188 Tongue Farm Rd	Matakana
La Pineta Vineyards Ltd	Michael Hinchco	09 422 7200	PO Box 609	Warkworth
Leigh Fisheries	Greg Bishop	09 422 6424		RD5 Warkworth
Leigh Sawmill Brewery	Peter Freckleton	09 422 6555	142 Pakiri Road	Leigh
Lothlorien Orchards	Dale Meulemeester	09 422 5846	1227 Ahuroa Rd RD1	Warkworth
Mahurangi River Vineyard	Colin McDonald	09 425 0306	162 Hamilton Rd RD2	Warkworth
Mahurangi Harbour Oyster Growers group	Andrew & Lisa Hay	09 425 5652	Ridge Road	Mahurangi
Matakana Chillies	Sandra Bollard & Tom Greenwood	09 422 7519	RD5	Warkworth

EMAIL	WEB	CATEGORY
andbina@woosh.co.nz		Garlic
ascension@xtra.co.nz	www.ascensionvineyard.co.nz	Winery
rachel@oleanz.co.nz	www.oleanz.co.nz	Winery
jim@biomarine.co.nz	www.biomarine.co.nz	Biobusiness
shannon@blue.co.nz	www.blue.co.nz	Icecream, blueberries
wines@brickbay.co.nz	www.brickbay.co.nz	Winery
contourestate@xtra.co.nz	www.contourestate.co.nz	Winery
info@devinechocolat.co.nz		Chocolate
teresa@echovalleyolives.co.nz		Olives
elocinfoods@xtra.co.nz	www.elocinfoods.co.nz	Gluten-free bakery
ffenz@ihug.co.nz		Food
peter@greve.co.nz	www.greve.co.nz	Winery
hawksnestorchard@xtra.co.nz		Wine, persimmons, avocadoes, mandarins, limes, cherimoyas
winemakerscentre@heronsflight.co.nz	www.heronsflight.co.nz	Winery
katiemitchell@xtra.co.nz	www.mahurangiduck.co.nz	Ducks
wigglesworth@clear.net.nz		Table/dessert grapes, strawberries, raspberries
hinchco_wines@xtra.co.nz		Winery
	www.homefresh.com	Grower and retail
info@honeycentre.co.nz		Honey
john@hyperion-wines.co.nz	www.hyperion-wines.co.nz	Winery
hinchco_wines@xtra.co.nz		Winery
greg@leefish.co.nz		Seafood
brewery@eei.co.nz	www.sawmillbrewery.co.nz	Food & beverage
		Organics — fruit wine and juice
tony@mahurangiriver.co.nz	www.mahurangiriver.co.nz	Winery
kawauoysters@xtra.co.nz		Oysters
sandra@matakanachillies.co.nz	www.matakanachillies.co.nz	Chillies

GROWERS AND PRODUCERS

BUSINESS NAME	CONTACT	PHONE	ADDRESS	AREA
Matakana Estate	Ros Brown	09 425 0494	568 Matakana Road	Matakana
Matakana Farmers Market	Michael Kessel	09 422 6889	Matakana Valley Road	Matakana
Matakana Olive Co-operative Ltd	Murray Jardine	09 422 3248	PO Box 95	Matakana
Matakana Patisserie	Tyrone & Delwyn Vincent	09 422 9896	70 Matakana Valley Road	Matakana
Matakana Smokehouse	Pete & Kim Clementson	09 422 9575	988 Matakana Road	Matakana
Matakana Valley Organics	Linda Porteous	09 423 7404	960 Matakana Valley Road	Matakana
Mustardmakers Ltd	Jon & Morag Standbrook	09 422 0069	18 Ahuroa Road	Puhoi
Olives	Silvana Silvestro & Mike Dodds	021 688 263	57 Quintal Rd RD5	Matakana
Omaha Bay Vineyard	Beverly & Hegman Foster	09 423 0022	189 Takatu Road	Matakana
Omaha Blueberries Ltd	Robert & Shannon Auton	09 422 9886	89 Jones Rd	Omaha
Pacific Blueberries Ltd		09 422 7978	242A Omaha Road	Omaha
Pak Thai	John & Wiwan Hay		Matakana Road	Matakana
Providence Vineyards Ltd	James Vuletic	09 444 6064	45 Takatu Rd	Omaha
Puhoi Valley Cheese Co		09 422 0619	275 Ahuroa Road	Puhoi
Rainbow Valley Farm	Trish Allen	09 422 7432		Matakana
Ransom Wines	Robin & Marion Ransom	09 425 8862	46 Valerie Close	Warkworth
Saltings Estate Vineyard	Maureen & Terry Baines	09 425 9670	1210 Sandspit Rd	Sandspit
Salumeria Fontana Ltd	Greg Scopas			Matakana
Southern Paprika	Hamish Alexander	09 425 9496	PO Box 614	Warkworth
Southern Seafoods International Ltd		09 422 9782	PO Box 62	Matakana
Stubbs Village Butchery	James & Rebecca McCarthy	09 422 9650	2 Matakana Valley Road	Matakana
Takatu Vineyard & Lodge	Heather & John Forsman	09 423 0299	518 Whitmore Rd	Matakana
Tamahanga Gardens	Bridget Ledbrook		Omaha Valley Road	Omaha
Taste	Mike & Andrea Hinchco	09 425 0302	4 Neville Street	Warkworth
The Art of Cheese	Chris & Nicole Leuthold	09 422 0670	275 Ahuroa Rd	Puhoi
The Castle Matakana	Val Sutherland	09 422 9288	378 Whitmore Rd	Matakana
The Matakana Fresh Food Co.	Andrew Steens & Angela Wain			Omaha
The Vintry	Nicki Haller	09 423 0251	Matakana Valley Road	Matakana 0948
Ti Point Vineyard	Jan Haslam	09 422 6908	Cnr Ti Point and Tairere Rds	Ti Point
Waybyond Organics	Jeni Quayle	09 423 8474	177 Wayby Station Rd RD2	Wellsford

EMAIL	WEB	CATEGORY
cellar@matakanaestate.co.nz		Winery
mihou@paradise.net.nz		Farmers' market
matakanaolives@gmail.com		Olives
delwyn@matakanapatisserie.co.nz		Patisserie
matakanasmokehouse@xtra.co.nz		Smoked salmon, mussels, meats, & veges
matakanavalleyorganics@ihug.co.nz		Vegetables
info@mustardmakers.co.nz	www.mustardmakers.co.nz	Mustards
silvanas@xtra.co.nz		Olives
omahabay@xtra.co.nz	www.omahabay.co.nz	Winery
omahablueberries@xtra.co.nz	www.blue.co.nz	Blueberries
		Blueberries
		Asian vegetables
jvuletic@orcon.co.nz		Winery
franck.beaurain@goodmanfielder.co.nz		Cheese
	www.rainbowvalleyfarm.co.nz	Organics
info@ransomwines.co.nz	www.ransomwines.co.nz	Winery
relax@saltings.co.nz	www.saltings.co.nz	Olives, winery
		Artisan sausages
hamishalexander@southernpaprika.co.nz	www.southernpaprika.co.nz	Biobusiness
info@seafood.co.nz		Seafood
tabitha@stubbsvillagebutchery.co.nz	www.stubbsvillagebutchery.co.nz	Butcher & deli
info@takatuwine.co.nz	www.takatuwine.co.nz	Winery
info@tamahunga-gardens.co.nz		Vegetables
hinchco_wines@xtra.co.nz		Farmers' food store
artofcheese@xtra.co.nz	www.artofcheesecafe.co.nz	Cheese
mail@the-castle.co.nz	www.the-castle.co.nz	Winery
		Vegetables
nickiaych@yahoo.com		Wine
jan@tipointretreat.co.nz		Winery
jquayle@ihug.co.nz		Organic vegetables, herbs

ACCOLADES AND BOUQUETS

Many thanks to all the people who helped me fall in love with Matakana and Omaha.

I would never have realised how great Omaha was if it wasn't for the hospitality of Maxine and John Bayley at their former beach house. They inspired us to build our own special place.

Christine and Richard Didsbury shared their vision and have made the district a world-class rural community.

And thanks to my many friends at Omaha Beach who often propped me up with a drink when I needed to escape from my work and acted as guinea pigs for my test recipes.

I love all the food producers of the area. It's the farmers, artisan producers and regulars at the Matakana farmers' market who have provided the inspiration for this book. Rain or shine, it's always exciting to visit the market on Saturdays and buy fresh produce so I can spend the weekend cooking treats for friends and family.

Special thanks to some who went out of their way to ensure I had the freshest and best produce for my recipes: Greg and Kath for their sausages, Jeni for the eggs, Pete for the smoked salmon, Lynette and Trevor for the oysters, Rachel Taulelei of Yellow Brick Road for the Leigh snapper, James of Stubbs Village Butchery for the lamb and beef, John and Wi for herbs, Andrew for beans and heritage tomatoes, and Shannon for the blueberries.

I'm so grateful to Kathy Paterson, a wonderful cook, who helped me prepare the food to be photographed. She's the best.

Ken Downie is a conscientious photographer with a wonderful eye who has truly captured Matakana — and even enjoyed my food.

It's always a pleasure to work with the wonderful team at Random House who have faith in my ideas: Nicola Legat, Leonie Freeman and Jennifer Balle.

Thanks to Toni Mason for her skilled editing and Karryn Muschamp, designer with flair. I have loved working with both these talented people at *Cuisine* and working on a book has been just as much fun.

For historical reference I used *Jade River: A History of the Mahurangi* by RH Locker, published by Friends of the Mahurangi (2007), and 'Matakana History', a research paper by Tania Mace (2003), commissioned and kindly loaned by Brick Bay Trust.

And much gratitude to the team at the Rodney Economic Development Trust, who also believed in this project and were so helpful.

For further information: www.warkworthnz.com; www.rodney.govt.nz; www.matakanavillage.co.nz; www.matakanawine.com

....

ABOUT THE AUTHOR AND PHOTOGRAPHER

LAURAINE JACOBS is one of New Zealand's best-known and most ardent champions of good produce, great cooking and superb restaurants. During her longstanding career as food editor of *Cuisine* magazine she has established international connections with leading culinary professionals and acts as an important food and wine ambassador for New Zealand. Her most recent book is the popular cookbook *The Confident Cook*. She lives in Auckland but spends as much time as she can at her holiday house at Omaha Beach.

KEN DOWNIE is an Auckland photographer whose work appears frequently in *Cuisine*, *Metro* and *North & South* magazines.